Published by
Ooey Gooey, Inc.
Rochester, New York
All Rights Reserved

Published by Ooey Gooey, Inc.
Rochester, New York
www.ooeygooey.com

ISBN # 978-0-9706634-3-6

First printing: 2010 in Singapore
Second printing: 2012 in United States

Printed on recycled paper using soy based ink.

Acknowledgements and Creative Credit:

Cover design and book formatting and layout by Andrew Curl of Drew Design, San Diego, CA.
Back cover photograph of the author by CéCé Canton, San Diego, CA.
Handprints Poem #3 courtesy of Jen McSweeney, Rochester, NY.
"He who owns the language owns the debate" quote provided by Dr. Elizabeth Waller, Fairport, NY.
Inside Illustrations by Todd Rohnke, Rochester, NY.
Cover photograph of toddler in colored spaghetti taken by Kimberly Hornberg, Tuscon, AZ.
Back cover photos and all inside photos are courtesy of the author.

Front cover activity is **COLORED SPAGHETTI** which appears in Lisa's first book, *The Ooey Gooey® Handbook*. We accidentally forgot to include it in *Ooey Gooey® Tooey*!

You make colored spaghetti by cooking the pasta just like you are going to eat it, but add 1 cup of oil to the water when you boil the noodles! Cook it, strain it, color the cooked pasta with liquid watercolor or food coloring and then put the colored pasta in your sensory tub! **Enjoy!**

There are two ways of spreading light.
To be the candle or the mirror that reflects it.

Edith Wharton

Once Again,
For Tom.
I love you way high to the moon.

ANOTHER NOTE TO YOU FROM LISA

I will be very honest with you... I didn't want to write just another activity book. Simply doing activities with children does not make us good teachers. Thoughtful and intentional planning of these activities, partnered with passion, sprinkled with commitment and served up with some honest to goodness dedication to the field of early childhood education is what makes us good teachers. Having a repertoire of activities at our disposal is a natural by-product of this passion. The activities we plan might serve as an indicator of our creativity and our desire to provide opportunities for children that they might not get to do anywhere else, but the truth of the matter is that it does not matter how much playdough we know how to make if we don't like our jobs. Activities do not sustain, nor do they accurately reflect the true quality of our child care programs. The budget for materials and supplies could go away and (believe it or not) we'd all be fine as long as the school was still filled with people who had a passion in their belly and fire in their souls. But you know this. And while I could banter educational philosophy back and forth with you all day long, you asked for another book, so here you go; another book! Most of what has been collected here are variations of popular activities children and adults have been doing together since forever. Many of them are from my college years and my first few years of teaching. I blew the dust off some of those first few lesson plan books and found a few gems. I doubt any of the activities contained in these pages are "new" in the sense of "no one has ever done this before!" But many of them might be new to you, and that is the idea. Some of the ideas were shared with me via emails, phone calls and in the back of the room after a conference. Some of them I watched others do, some were created by the children, some of them I observed in the classrooms at our Playschool and some of them I simply heard about so we tinkered around the kitchen until we got it right.   Regardless, I wrote them down, collected them, saved them and stored them for the past eight-or-so years. Then in early 2008 I revisited this hodge-podge collection and began deciphering the chicken scratch and reading through the ideas that had been hurriedly scribbled on the back of napkins and on scraps of paper. We had accumulated quite a pile, more than one-hundred actually. So we decided to get to work. Again, please let me restate that I could not have compiled this assortment of ideas if not for the workshop attendees, friends, Ooey Gooey® Members, Ooey Gooey® Summer Session participants, mentors and other kind and generous folks who made sure to send me their latest discoveries and concoctions. *Ooey Gooey® Tooey* would not exist if not for you and your willingness to take a minute to share with me what you were up to.

It is said that the holy trinity of Cajun cooking consists of bell pepper, onion and celery.   I think the holy trinity (plus two) of preschool/child care activities consists of:

1) Flubber
2) Playdough
3) Knox® Gelatin Molds
4) Bubbles
5) Ooblick

And because of this, these five recipes/activities have appeared in my other two activity books as well as also appearing here. Sometimes we can only afford one book at a time, and I want to make sure that everyone who makes the investment in one of my activity books gets what I consider to be the "classic" activities. So with the exception of the five activities listed above, and unless an activity from one of my other books has been significantly modified, improved or is now just so earth shatteringly different that it just had to be included, the activities contained herein *Ooey Gooey® Tooey* did not appear in either *The Ooey Gooey® Handbook* or *Fizzle Bubble Pop and Wow.*

The "Wolf Words" do appear again though. This was one of the biggest requests when I started mentioning that I was working on "a new book." Many of you asked for the Wolf Words again, so we provided those for you too. We trust that eventually (When?! Please! When??) we won't have to include them in all the activity books and on every handout, but alas, unfortunately at this time, we still do.

For the uninitiated, the Wolf Words are the "concept words", sometimes called the "learning words" that one could attach to an activity when someone comes into the room and demands, "What are they doing?" or, "What are they learning?" I have the most success in speaking with wolves when I use a "verbing the noun" formula. Without spending too much time repeating information which appears elsewhere in my other writings, I will provide this "in a nutshell" advice to new readers: the most informative way to phrase what the children are "doing" is to inform the wolves that the children are verbing the noun and that such verbing assists in developing or strengthening XYZ. For example: The children are stacking the blocks, and such stacking assists in fine motor coordination which leads to writing skills. In shorthand, stacking blocks = prewriting! Bam! Wolf Words in Action! For those of you who really want more, I will refer you to my article entitled "A Crash Course in the Language of Wolves" which is available in the "resources" section of my website www.ooeygooey.com. And until such time that our culture embraces the belief that as teachers we know what we are doing and we no longer need to defend our work with children, I will urge you to remember this:

He who owns the language owns the debate. If knowing the Wolf Words keeps flubber, playdough, crayons, parachutes, sensory tubs, easels and blocks in our toddler and preschool rooms then we have a responsibility to know them. We might wish we didn't have to, but if our intention is to put theory into action and to do what we know is good practice and if knowing that by squeezing and squishing playdough a child is strengthening the last muscle in her hand that needs to be strong before she can hold a pencil, we have a professional obligation to be able to articulate these facts and connections. When tossed on a table for independent exploration, playdough will be squished, rolled, molded and twisted into various designs and shapes. And truth be told, children will figure things out about playdough whether or not an adult is sitting next to them. And while there must be room for this style of independent exploration and freedom, it also needs to be stated that when playdough is set out as an activity with intention and as a conscious choice by the teacher in this room for the children in this room the entire experience takes on a level that goes much deeper than, "We always have the playdough out at center time." When playdough, or any activity for that matter, is facilitated by conscientious, caring and loving adults who are committed to understanding the ongoing link between play, theory, learning and practice, the entire educational process becomes a much more meaningful experience for students and teachers alike. As early childhood educators, we constantly have to defend the importance of playing for plays sake while also being expected to talk about the importance of what the children are "learning" when they are engaged in such free play. The problem with this expectation is that it continues to perpetuate the myth that somehow there is a difference between living, learning and playing. Many of you are quite well aware of my position on this. I am enraged that at this day and age we still have to constantly defend what has already been proven. The research proving the importance of play in the cognitive, social, physical and emotional development has already been done. When will we finally be able to put it into practice instead of having to defend it? Then and only then will we stop reinforcing the incorrect belief that play is somehow separate from learning.

In conclusion I wish to say that I make no claim to inventing or creating any of the recipes contained herein. I have tried each and every one of them, but did not invent any of them. The names of the activities and ideas which I include here are the names given to them by the folks who shared them with me and all efforts were made to make sure we did not infringe on any trademarks or copyrights. If, however, something was missed or unintentionally overlooked, we ask that you bring it to our attention at the address on the back information page so future additions can be corrected and proper credit given. And there we go. I think that's enough for now. I will save more philosophy talk for the next book. For now, let's go play. But before we do, please, once again allow me to thank you from the bottom of my heart for your continued support of our adventures and of our message of the importance of play in the lives of our children. We absolutely would not be where we are today without you.

All my best,

CONTENTS

PLAYDOUGH
RECIPES

BASIC PLAYDOUGH

You Need: 3 cups flour
1 ½ cups salt
6 tsp cream of tartar
6 TBS oil
3 cups water
Liquid Water Color or food coloring (optional)
Bowl
Electric Mixer (or a hand whisk)
Wooden spoon

Directions:

Using an electric mixer, mix all ingredients together in a bowl. You can mix with a big spoon or a hand whisk if you don't have an electric mixer. Cook over medium heat until it forms a ball. Remove from heat, knead. Store in a baggie or air tight container.

From the Ooey Gooey® Test Kitchens:

This is hands-down, the best playdough recipe ever.

Small Motor Skills

Spatial Skills

Counting

Measuring

Social Skills

Chemistry

Color Mixing

Creativity

Language Development

Sensory Skills

Use of Tools

Comparing and Contrasting

COFFEE PLAYDOUGH

You Need: 3 cups flour

1 ½ cups salt

6 tsp cream of tartar

6 TBS oil

3 cups water

Wet coffee grounds from the morning coffee (I use all the grounds in the filter basket that were used from making a full pot of coffee)

Bowl

Electric Mixer (or a hand whisk)

Wooden spoon

Directions:

Using an electric mixer, mix all ingredients together in a bowl. You can mix with a big spoon or a hand whisk if you don't have an electric mixer. Cook over medium heat until it forms a ball. Remove from heat, knead. Store in a baggie or air tight container.

From the Ooey Gooey® Test Kitchens:

The neat thing about coffee dough is that the coffee grounds provide a smell, texture and color to the playdough!

Small Motor Skills

Spatial Skills

Counting

Measuring

Social Skills

Chemistry

Color Mixing

Creativity

Language Development

Sensory Skills

Use of Tools

Comparing and Contrasting

CHOCOLATE PLAYDOUGH

You Need: 2 cups flour
1 ½ cups salt
⅔ cups cocoa powder
6 tsp cream of tartar
6 TBS oil
3 cups water
Bowl
Electric Mixer (or a hand whisk)
Wooden spoon

Small Motor Skills

Spatial Skills

Counting

Measuring

Social Skills

Chemistry

Color Mixing

Creativity

Language Development

Sensory Skills

Use of Tools

Comparing and Contrasting

Directions:
Using an electric mixer, mix all ingredients together in a bowl. If it looks a little dry, add a little bit more water. You can mix with a big spoon or a hand whisk if you don't have an electric mixer. Cook over medium heat until it forms a ball. Remove from heat, knead. Store in a baggie or air tight container.

Reality Check:
Someone is going to tell you what they think it looks like. Think about it. Yes. It looks like that. Get over it. You can't be like, "Hey! There is no poop here!" because that would be lying. If you run around saying "Don't say poop!" they are going to say it because now they know it bugs you!

STRAWBERRY CAKE PLAYDOUGH

You Need: 1 package strawberry cake mix (any brand)
2 cups flour
1 ½ cups salt
6 tsp cream of tartar
6 TBS oil
3 cups water
Bowl
Electric Mixer (or a hand whisk)
Wooden spoon

Small Motor Skills
Spatial Skills
Counting
Measuring
Social Skills
Chemistry
Color Mixing
Creativity
Language Development
Sensory Skills
Use of Tools
Comparing and Contrasting

Directions:

Using an electric mixer, mix all ingredients together in a bowl. If it looks a little dry, add a little bit more water. You can mix with a big spoon or a hand whisk if you don't have an electric mixer. Cook over medium heat until it forms a ball. Remove from heat, knead. Store in a baggie or air tight container.

Optional:

You can add some additional red coloring to make the color brighter if desired.

LEMON POPPY SEED PLAYDOUGH

You Need: 1 package lemon poppy seed muffin (or cake) mix (any brand)
2 cups flour
1 ½ cups salt
6 tsp cream of tartar
6 TBS oil
3 cups water
Bowl
Electric Mixer (or a hand whisk)
Wooden spoon

Small Motor Skills

Spatial Skills

Counting

Measuring

Social Skills

Chemistry

Color Mixing

Creativity

Language Development

Sensory Skills

Use of Tools

Comparing and Contrasting

Directions:
Using an electric mixer, mix all ingredients together in a bowl. If it looks a little dry, add a little bit more water. You can mix with a big spoon or a hand whisk if you don't have an electric mixer. Cook over medium heat until it forms a ball. Remove from heat, knead. Store in a baggie or air tight container.

Optional:
You can add some additional yellow coloring to make the color brighter if desired.

20

GLITTER PLAYDOUGH

You Need: 3 cups flour
1 ½ cups salt
6 tsp cream of tartar
6 TBS oil
3 cups water
Glitter
Liquid Water Color or food coloring (optional)
Bowl
Electric Mixer (or a hand whisk)
Wooden spoon

Directions:
Using an electric mixer, mix all ingredients together in a bowl. You can mix with a big spoon or a hand whisk if you don't have an electric mixer. Cook over medium heat until it forms a ball. Remove from heat, knead for awhile and then add some glitter. Store in a baggie or air tight container.

From the Ooey Gooey® Test Kitchens:
Testers really enjoyed making playdough with black liquid water coloring and silver glitter for a true silver and black attack!

Small Motor Skills
Spatial Skills
Counting
Measuring
Social Skills
Chemistry
Color Mixing
Creativity
Language Development
Sensory Skills
Use of Tools
Comparing and Contrasting

PUMPKIN BREAD PLAYDOUGH

You Need: 1 package pumpkin bread mix (any brand)
2 cups flour
1 ½ cups salt
6 tsp cream of tartar
6 TBS oil
3 cups water
Bowl
Electric Mixer (or a hand whisk)
Wooden spoon

Small Motor Skills

Spatial Skills

Counting

Measuring

Social Skills

Chemistry

Color Mixing

Creativity

Language Development

Sensory Skills

Use of Tools

Comparing and Contrasting

Directions:
Using an electric mixer, mix all ingredients together in a bowl. If it looks a little dry, add a little bit more water. You can mix with a big spoon or a hand whisk if you don't have an electric mixer. Cook over medium heat until it forms a ball. Remove from heat, knead. Store in a baggie or air tight container.

From the Ooey Gooey® Test Kitchens:
We thought you could almost smell the change of seasons while playing with this one. Smells like Autumn!

PUMPKIN PIE PLAYDOUGH

You Need: 3 cups flour
1 ½ cups salt
6 tsp cream of tartar
6 tsp pumpkin pie spice
1 ½ tsp cinnamon
6 TBS oil
3 cups water
Bowl
Electric Mixer (or a hand whisk)
Wooden spoon

Small Motor Skills

Spatial Skills

Counting

Measuring

Social Skills

Chemistry

Color Mixing

Creativity

Language Development

Sensory Skills

Use of Tools

Comparing and Contrasting

Directions:
Using an electric mixer, mix all ingredients together in a bowl. You can mix with a big spoon or a hand whisk if you don't have an electric mixer. Cook over medium heat until it forms a ball. Remove from heat, knead. Store in a baggie or air tight container.

From the Ooey Gooey® Test Kitchens:
A couple testers wondered if you could put whipped cream on it! We had to remind them it was playdough time, not snack time!

SOOTHING PLAYDOUGH

Small Motor Skills

Spatial Skills

Counting

Measuring

Social Skills

Chemistry

Color Mixing

Creativity

Language Development

Sensory Skills

Use of Tools

Comparing and Contrasting

You Need: 5 cups flour
3 TBS powdered alum (in the spice aisle)
¾ cup salt
6 TBS oil
3 cups water
1 cup (any brand) lavender chamomile baby lotion
Liquid Water Color or food coloring (optional)
Bowl
Electric Mixer (or a hand whisk)
Wooden spoon

Directions:

Using an electric mixer, mix all ingredients together in a bowl. If it looks a little dry, add a little bit more water. You can mix with a big spoon or a hand whisk if you don't have an electric mixer. Cook over medium heat until it forms a ball. Remove from heat, knead. If it looks a little sticky while kneading, add some flour (2 TBS or so) and continue kneading. Store in a baggie or air tight container.

From the Ooey Gooey® Test Kitchens:

This one was so very creamy and very,very soft and soothing.

GINGERBREAD PLAYDOUGH

You Need: 1 package gingerbread mix (any brand)
2 cups flour
1 ½ cups salt
6 tsp cream of tartar
6 TBS oil
3 cups water
Bowl
Electric Mixer (or a hand whisk)
Wooden spoon

Directions:

Using an electric mixer, mix all ingredients together in a bowl. If it looks a little dry, add a little bit more water. You can mix with a big spoon or a hand whisk if you don't have an electric mixer. Cook over medium heat until it forms a ball. Remove from heat, knead. Store in a baggie or air tight container.

Small Motor Skills

Spatial Skills

Counting

Measuring

Social Skills

Chemistry

Color Mixing

Creativity

Language Development

Sensory Skills

Use of Tools

Comparing and Contrasting

CORNSTARCH PLAYDOUGH

You Need: 2 cups baking soda
1 ½ cups water
1 cup cornstarch
Liquid Water Color or food coloring (optional)
Saucepan
Wooden Spoon

Small Motor Skills

Spatial Skills

Counting

Measuring

Social Skills

Chemistry

Color Mixing

Creativity

Language Development

Sensory Skills

Use of Tools

Comparing and Contrasting

Directions:
Mix all ingredients together in a saucepan. Bring to a boil over medium heat and cook until thick. Remove from heat, knead. If the dough is too sticky add a little flour or some extra cornstarch while kneading. Store in a baggie or air tight container.

Double or triple the recipe based on the amount required.

From the Ooey Gooey® Test Kitchens:
This was a huge hit with everyone who played with it!

PIZZA PLAYDOUGH

You Need: 2 cups flour
1 ½ cups cornmeal
1 ½ cups salt
6 tsp cream of tartar
2 TBS garlic powder
2 TBS basil
2 TBS oregano
6 TBS oil
3 ½ cups water
Bowl
Electric Mixer (or a hand whisk)
Wooden spoon

Small Motor Skills
Spatial Skills
Counting
Measuring
Social Skills
Chemistry
Color Mixing
Creativity
Language Development
Sensory Skills
Use of Tools
Comparing and Contrasting

Directions:

Using an electric mixer, mix all ingredients together in a bowl. If it looks a little dry, add a little bit more water. You can mix with a big spoon or a hand whisk if you don't have an electric mixer. Cook over medium heat until it forms a ball. Remove from heat, knead. Store in a baggie or air tight container.

From the Ooey Gooey® Test Kitchens:

Tom tried to eat this one…. Step away from the table Mr. Murphy!

MICROWAVE PLAYDOUGH

You Need: 2 cups flour
1 cup salt
4 tsp cream of tartar
2 cups water
3 TBS oil
Liquid Water Color or food coloring (optional)
Bowl
Wooden spoon

Directions:
Mix all the ingredients together in a microwave safe bowl. Cook on high heat in the microwave for 2 ½ minutes. Stir vigorously and then cook on high heat for 2 more minutes. Knead, but be careful! It will be really hot! Store in a baggie or air tight container.

Small Motor Skills

Spatial Skills

Counting

Measuring

Social Skills

Chemistry

Color Mixing

Creativity

Language Development

Sensory Skills

Use of Tools

Comparing and Contrasting

SALTY MODELING DOUGH

You Need: ⅔ cup water
2 cups salt
½ cup water
1 cup cornstarch
Saucepan
Wooden Spoon
An extra bowl

Directions:

In a saucepan over medium heat mix the ⅔ cup water and 2 cups salt. Cook and stir over medium heat for about 3-4 minutes. It will start to get very thick and salty. Remove from heat.

In a separate bowl mix the ½ cup water and 1 cup cornstarch and stir. Add this cornstarch mixture to the first salt and water mixture you made on the stove. Put it back on the stove on low heat and stir until smooth. The dough will thicken quickly. Remove from heat and knead. You can use it the same way as you use playdough or you can make designs to dry and save. It is a thicker dough and will dry easily in the sun.

Small Motor Skills
Spatial Skills
Counting
Measuring
Social Skills
Chemistry
Color Mixing
Creativity
Language Development
Sensory Skills
Use of Tools
Comparing and Contrasting

SOAPY STRETCHY PLAYDOUGH

You need to break this process into 2 parts:

Small Motor Skills

Spatial Skills

Counting

Measuring

Social Skills

Chemistry

Color Mixing

Creativity

Language Development

Sensory Skills

Use of Tools

Comparing and Contrasting

PART 1   4 TBS salt
½ cup liquid starch
1 cup liquid soap ** (see Test Kitchen comments on the next page)
⅛ cup water
1 TBS glue (any brand)
2 cups cornmeal
A big bowl
Wooden spoon

PART 2   ½ cup glue (any brand)
1½ cups cornmeal

Directions:

In a big bowl, mix all the ingredients in **PART 1**.
Then in the same bowl add the ingredients from **PART 2**.

Continue mixing everything together. You can use this in the same manner you would use playdough or you can put it out in your sensory tub. It does leave a soapy, cornmeal residue on your hands. Notice when you wash your hands that you make extra soapy bubbles in the sink!

From the Ooey Gooey® Test Kitchens:

We made three test batches with three different kinds of soap. One with Dawn®, one with Palmolive® (lavender scented) and one with Ajax® (orange scented). We liked the feeling and consistency of the mixture made with Palmolive®, some of the teachers said they preferred the Dawn®.

Also, this was a hit when used on the table like a "dough" *and* when we doubled it (and tripled it!) for an activity in the sensory tubs.

GLUTEN/WHEAT FREE PLAYDOUGH
VARIATION #1

Small Motor Skills

Spatial Skills

Counting

Measuring

Social Skills

Chemistry

Color Mixing

Creativity

Language Development

Sensory Skills

Use of Tools

Comparing and Contrasting

You Need: 1 ½ cups rice flour

1 ½ cups cornstarch

1 ½ cups salt

6 tsp cream of tartar

3 cups water

3 tsp oil

Liquid Water Color or food coloring (optional)

Bowl

Electric Mixer (or a hand whisk)

Wooden spoon

Directions:

Using an electric mixer, mix all ingredients together in a bowl. You can mix with a big spoon or a hand whisk if you don't have an electric mixer. Cook over medium heat until it forms a ball. Remove from heat, knead. Store in a baggie or air tight container.

GLUTEN/WHEAT FREE PLAYDOUGH
VARIATION #2

You Need: 2 cups rice flour
2 cups salt
1 TBS cream of tartar
2 TBS cooking oil
1 ¾ cups water
Liquid Water Color or food coloring (optional)
Bowl
Electric Mixer (or a hand whisk)
Wooden spoon

Directions:
Using an electric mixer, mix all ingredients together in a bowl. You can mix with a big spoon or a hand whisk if you don't have an electric mixer. Cook over medium heat until it forms a ball. Remove from heat, knead. Store in a baggie or air tight container.

Small Motor Skills

Spatial Skills

Counting

Measuring

Social Skills

Chemistry

Color Mixing

Creativity

Language Development

Sensory Skills

Use of Tools

Comparing and Contrasting

NO FLOUR PLAYDOUGH

You Need: 2 cups cornstarch
1 cup salt
1 TBS shortening
1 ½ cups water
½ TBS oil
Liquid Water Color or food coloring (optional)
Bowl
Electric Mixer (or a hand whisk)
Wooden spoon

Directions:
Using an electric mixer, mix all ingredients together in a bowl. You can mix with a big spoon or a hand whisk if you don't have an electric mixer. Cook over medium heat until it forms a ball. Remove from heat, knead. Store in a baggie or air tight container.

Small Motor Skills

Spatial Skills

Counting

Measuring

Social Skills

Chemistry

Color Mixing

Creativity

Language Development

Sensory Skills

Use of Tools

Comparing and Contrasting

FLUBBER

and

SLIME

RECIPES

BASIC FLUBBER

You Need: 3 TBS Borax
1 cup glue
4 cups warm water
2 bowls (1 large & 1 small)
Wooden spoon
Liquid Water Color or food coloring (optional)

Directions:
In a bowl mix together:
2 cups warm water
1 cup glue
Food coloring or liquid water color

In a separate smaller bowl mix together:
2 cups warm water
3 TBS Borax

Now S L O W L Y and a little at a time, pour the Borax mixture into the glue mixture. Stir with your fingers. You will feel the Borax water start to coagulate the glue. Keep pouring S L O W L Y until the flubber has reached the desired consistency.

Small Motor Skills

Counting

Measuring

Social Skills

Science

Chemistry (Suspensions)

Reactions

Color Mixing

Creativity

Language Development

Sensory Awareness

Use of Tools

Comparing and Contrasting

Observation Skills

A couple of important notes:

1) Do not just pour the Borax water all in at once. It will turn rock hard, will not be stretchy and you will be upset.

2) You probably will NOT need all of the Borax water that you made.

3) Store the flubber in a Ziploc® bag. It will last a few weeks. It does NOT need to be in the fridge.

4) Mayo will remove flubber from hair and Vinegar will remove it from things: couch, clothes, carpet, etc.

5) It is time for a new batch when the flubber starts breaking apart and is no longer very stretchy. I don't throw it away. Instead, I send a little bit home with each child (in a small zippie bag) with a copy of the recipe!

GLITTER FLUBBER

You Need: 3 TBS Borax
               1 cup glue
               4 cups warm water
               2 bowls (1 large & 1 small)
               Wooden spoon
               Glitter
               Liquid Water Color or food coloring (optional)

Directions:
In a bowl mix together:
2 cups warm water
1 cup glue
Some glitter
Food coloring or liquid water color

In a separate smaller bowl mix together:
2 cups warm water
3 TBS Borax

Small Motor Skills

Counting

Measuring

Social Skills

Science

Chemistry (Suspensions)

Reactions

Color Mixing

Creativity

Language Development

Sensory Awareness

Use of Tools

Comparing and Contrasting

Observation Skills

Now S L O W L Y and a little at a time, pour the Borax mixture into the glue mixture. Stir with your fingers. You will feel the Borax water start to coagulate the glue. Keep pouring S L O W L Y until the flubber has reached the desired consistency.

Remember that the "Important Notes" from the Basic Flubber recipe on page 37 still apply here!

CLEAR FLUBBER

You Need: 3 TBS Borax
1 cup clear glue
4 ½ cups warm water
2 bowls (1 large & 1 small)
Wooden spoon

Directions:
In a bowl mix together:
2 ½ cups warm water
1 cup CLEAR glue

In a separate smaller bowl mix together:
2 cups warm water
3 TBS Borax

Small Motor Skills

Counting

Measuring

Social Skills

Science

Chemistry (Suspensions)

Reactions

Color Mixing

Creativity

Language Development

Sensory Awareness

Use of Tools

Comparing and Contrasting

Observation Skills

Now S L O W L Y and a little at a time, pour the Borax mixture into the glue mixture. Stir with your fingers. You will feel the Borax water start to coagulate the glue. Keep pouring S L O W L Y until the flubber has reached the desired consistency. The flubber feels the same, is often a little bit stiffer, but has a clear translucent look to it.

Once again, the "Important Notes" from Basic Flubber recipe apply here as well.

From the Ooey Gooey® Test Kitchens:
We liked adding glitter to this clear flubber mixture as well! Hold it up to the window… can you see through it?

BLOWING A FLUBBER BUBBLE

You Need: Flubber
Straws

One of the best things to do with flubber is to blow a bubble.
There are two techniques:

Hand Held Flubber Bubbles:

1) Lay some of the flubber flat in your hand. Use a piece that is slightly bigger than your palm.

2) Lay the straw flat (parallel) on the flubber.

3) Bring the flubber up and around the base of the straw. I often tell folks to imagine that the flubber is a balloon and now they have to blow the balloon up with the straw. What would your fingers need to do?

4) Make sure there is a little bit of room between the end of the straw and the flubber.

5) One hand will be holding the butt of the flubber and your other hand will be holding the flubber in place around the straw.

6) You are ready to blow! Start slow! WOW! Remember that practice makes perfect… keep going if you don't get it the first few times.

Small Motor Development

Cooperation

Social Skills

Following Instructions

Language Development

Observation

Comparing and Contrasting

Science

Chemistry (Suspensions)

Reactions

Creativity

Sensory Awareness

Use of Tools

Air Pressure

Observation Skills

Table Top Flubber Bubbles:

1) Put some flubber on the table. About ¼ of the batch is a good amount to start with.

2) Lay the straw flat (parallel) under the flubber. You want about ½ the straw under the flubber and the other ½ sticking out the front. This is where you will blow it up. Make sure the straw is NOT emerging from the other side of the flubber!

3) Squat down so you are the same height as the straw and place your hands in a diamond shape on top of the flubber in order to keep the sides of the flubber on the table and so that the bubble has room and space to grow.

4) You are ready to blow! Start slow! WOW! Remember that practice makes perfect... keep going if you don't get it the first few times.

HANDHELD FLUBBER BUBBLE

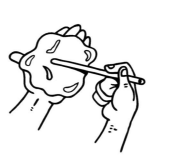  

TABLETOP FLUBBER BUBBLE

SLIME TIME

You Need: 2 TBS Metamucil®

2 ½ cups water

An empty, clean, jar with a lid (like a mayo or a mason jar)

Important Note Before Starting:

Metamucil® Slime is a time consuming project. It's worth it, but good to know on the front end that from start to finish this takes at least 90 minutes.

Directions:

Combine the Metamucil® and the water in the jar and shake for 2 minutes. Pour the contents of the jar into a microwave safe bowl and heat on high for about 5 minutes. Remove from the microwave and cool for about 3 minutes. Microwave again for about 5 minutes. Alternate the cooking and cooling process about four or five times.

After the forth or fifth cooking, allow the slime to cool for about an hour.

Two things from the Ooey Gooey® Test Kitchens:

1) Although much stickier than Flubber, the slime is of the same general consistency. It also registered a little higher on the children's "Grrroooosss!!" scale. This recipe makes enough for a classroom. If kept in an airtight zippie bag it will last about a week.

Small Motor Skills

Counting

Measuring

Social Skills

Science

Chemistry (Suspensions)

Reactions

Color Mixing

Creativity

Language Development

Sensory Awareness

Use of Tools

Comparing and Contrasting

Observation Skills

2) When we re-tested this for the book we could only find orange flavored Metamucil® so a couple of things happened: 1) the slime took on a natural orange coloring, so we did not add any additional coloring and 2) just an FYI: when playing with the slime our hands did get a little orange. No biggie. Just wanted to let you know.

Something to think about:

I enjoyed making a couple of batches and putting it in the sensory table instead of on the activity table. Sometimes the children become used to stickier stuff in the sensory tub and are more willing to try it out because that is "what it is for." Also, if you have children who have finally overcome their resistance to things like flubber and playdough, (which are typically "on the table" activities) you would want to be aware of the fact that slime is sticky and does stick to hands and fingers. That could possibly throw some kids a curve ball. Just something to keep in mind.

HANG IT UP!

Suspended flubber is one of the most exciting things to see when you walk into a classroom!

Hang any or all of the following and watch the reactions from the children:
- Colanders
- Strainers
- Funnels
- Berry Baskets
- Three-Tiered hanging fruit baskets
- Plastic food serving baskets (the ones with the holes in the sides)

Using sturdy string or twine, suspend any or an assortment of the above items from a secure spot in your ceiling or from the door frame. Place the whole batch of flubber in the top most basket and watch it come through.

You can hang up many single baskets, or suspend one basket on top of the other so it comes through one basket, then a second one, then a third one, etc...

Small Motor Skills

Counting

Measuring

Social Skills

Science

Chemistry (Suspensions)

Reactions

Color Mixing

Creativity

Language Development

Sensory Awareness

Use of Tools

Comparing and Contrasting

Observation Skills

SLIME FOR ONE

You Need: 1 tsp Metamucil®

1 cup water

An empty, clean, jar with a lid (like a mayo or a mason jar)

Directions:

Combine the Metamucil® and the water in the jar and shake for 60 seconds. Pour the contents of the jar into a microwave safe bowl and heat on high for about 5 minutes. Remove from the microwave and cool for about 3 minutes. Repeat the 5-minute cooking and 3-minute cooling process about 4 times.

Let the slime cool in the bowl for about an hour. Then stir it, knead it, roll it and play with it. It makes a small little baby batch of slime. Just enough for one. Store it in a zippie bag.

Observations from the Ooey Gooey® Test Kitchens:

When we tried to double this recipe we just didn't have good luck. It stayed very runny and never "gelled" (or is it "jelled?") together. Maybe you will have better luck than us. If you do – please let us know!

Small Motor Skills

Counting

Measuring

Social Skills

Science

Chemistry (Suspensions)

Reactions

Color Mixing

Creativity

Language Development

Sensory Awareness

Use of Tools

Comparing and Contrasting

Observation Skills

FLOAM

Small Motor Skills

Counting

Measuring

Social Skills

Science

Chemistry (Suspensions)

Reactions

Color Mixing

Creativity

Language Development

Sensory Awareness

Use of Tools

Comparing and Contrasting

Observation Skills

You Need: A batch of flubber

Polystyrene foam balls (bean bag filling)
I bought it from Uline www.uline.com but many
craft stores have it for sale too.

Directions:

To make homemade floam all you have to do is add about 2 cups of the small styrofoam balls to your flubber recipe. You can either mix them in while you are actually making the flubber or add them to the final product.

From the Ooey Gooey® Test Kitchens:

The environmentalists in the kitchen (myself included) cringed at the thought of using Styrofoam for anything, especially when it comes to clean up and disposal. Use common sense and be sensitive to environmental issues while still enjoying this activity!

From the Ooey Gooey® Test Kitchens:

We wondered how many batches of Floam we would have to make before we even made a dent in the huge bag of filler foam beads… Then we realized that you could use the foam filler to also make small pillows and beanbags! Brilliant!

MUD

Small Motor Skills

Volume/Mass

Math/Counting

Estimating

Saturation Point

Social Skills

Opposites (wet/dry)

Evaporation

Physical Changes

Chemical Reactions

Dramatic Play

Language Development

Sensory Awareness

Use of Tools

I know you are thinking, *"Really?! Mud?"* To which I will respond, "Yes! Mud!" Believe it or not, and for one reason or another, there are children who have never experienced what it is like to make real mud.

You Need: Dirt
Water
Pitchers

Directions:
Put a few buckets of dirt in your sensory tub. If you have access to what is called "clean, fill dirt" that would be great. But regular old dirt from the yard is fine. The best way to make good mud is to slowly add water to the dirt. So, I would suggest having dirt in your sensory tub and then on a nearby table having containers of water. Allow the children to scoop water in as needed. As the morning goes on you will have made mud. And it will be lovely.

Variation:

After the children have ample days of exploring the regular mud, you can spice it up by making Slippery Mud which is simply regular mud with a little bit of Liquid Starch and Dish Soap added to it. No "right" ratio. Add a little of each at a time and see what happens.

Caution:

Don't be in a hurry to make it into something different just for the sake of making it into something different. Especially if the kids have never even made real, regular basic mud before!

HOME MADE ICEBERGS

Small Motor Skills

Math/Measurement

Counting

Social Skills

Dramatic Play

Language Development

Sensory Awareness

Use of Tools

Opposites (wet/dry, liquid/solid)

Properties of water

Evaporation

Directions:

Freeze water in an assortment of interesting containers like:

- Ice cube trays with interesting shapes
- Film containers
- Cone shaped paper water cups
- Balloons
- Milk cartons (gallon sized and ½ gallon sized)
- Ziploc® Baggies
- Tupperware®
- Rubber gloves
- Plastic child-safe test tubes

And then put the frozen shapes in your sensory tub.

Variation:

Color the water prior to freezing if desired. Also, you can freeze small plastic animals, teddy bear counters, corks, marbles, barrel-of-monkey monkeys, etc. in the icebergs. How long does it take before the ice melts and you can retrieve the objects??

Safety Note:

When the frozen water balloon hits the surface of the water in the sensory tub the balloon material will pop. Safely discard the balloon remnants before the children play in the water table. Rubber gloves do not pop. It is fun to feel the ice melt inside the glove as the day goes on.

CANDLES AND SQUIRT BOTTLES
VARIATION #1

Hand-Eye Coordination

Safety Concepts

Math/Measurement

Counting

Estimating

Opposites (hot/cold)

We did this one year when we were doing lots of nursery rhymes. The children became fascinated with "Jack Be Nimble," consequently we stretched that rhyme into all corners of the classroom and into all areas of the curriculum. This became a fast favorite. But don't do this just for the novelty of lighting things on fire. Tie it into something meaningful and relevant for your group. You will know when it is appropriate.

You Need: Tall pillar candles

Matches

Squirt bottles filled with water

Directions:

Place some tall, thick, sturdy candles in your sensory tub. Not the ones in glass containers, but plain, tall, pillar candles. Provide hand held squirt bottles for the children. The idea is to squirt the flame out with the water from the squirt bottle.

From the Ooey Gooey® Test Kitchens:

Be aware of the overhead placement of fire alarms and smoke alarms. That's all I'm going to say about that. Be observant before just randomly lighting candles in the classroom! When in doubt, do it outside, on the patio, or driveway.

CANDLES AND SQUIRT BOTTLES
VARIATION #2

You Need: Floating tea light candles
Matches
Squirt bottles filled with water

Hand-Eye Coordination

Safety Concepts

Math/Measurement

Counting

Estimating

Opposites (hot/cold)

Directions:

This is a little harder. This time use floating tea lights. Fill your sensory tub with water and float some tea light candles on the top of the water. With the same hand held squirt bottles, squirt out the flames of the floating tea lights.

Was this easier or harder than Variation #1?

A SMALL SWAMP

Small Motor Skills

Math/Measurement

Counting

Social Skills

Opposites (wet/dry)

Dramatic Play

Language Development

Sensory Awareness

Use of Tools

In no regulated amount, size or design, add to your sensory tub any or all of the following:

> Mulch
> Peat Moss
> Rocks

You can either set it up dry or sprinkle a little bit of water on it.

A Story:

One year we made a swamp like this in our sensory tub and then someone painted on a big sheet of paper a swampy looking mixture of blue and green. After it dried, the children decided to tape the paper to the table and they put rocks and some dry moss around the image. So we had a "live" swamp in the tub and a painted one on the table. Remember to be open to the children's suggestions.

OOBLICK

Essentially Ooblick is equal parts of cornstarch and water. So if you measure out 5 boxes of cornstarch (approx. 10 cups) then you will need (approx.) 10 cups of water. But not always. Read on!

You Need: Cornstarch
Water

Small Motor Skills
Math/Counting
Estimating
Social Skills
Opposites (wet/dry)
Evaporation
Physical Changes
Chemical Reactions
Dramatic Play
Language Development
Sensory Awareness
Use of Tools

Directions:
Dump the cornstarch into your sensory tub. Slowly pour some water in and start mixing it all up. You might not need all of the water! You might need more water. Take your time.

From the Ooey Gooey® Test Kitchens:
As you get more comfortable and confident with your ooblick making abilities you will no longer need to measure. You will dump some cornstarch into your sensory tub and then add the necessary amount of water. Your hands will know when it's "right." Until then, measure it out but remember this: You will NOT always use all of the water. Meaning, if you have scooped out 20 cups of cornstarch, you might NOT need the full 20 cups of water. So be sure to add the water slowly. Otherwise you will need more starch, and then more water, and then more starch, and before you know it you have the, *"Oops! What happened to my bangs?"* haircut syndrome. Know what I mean?

OOBLICK WITH SHAVING CREAM

You Need: Ooblick
Shaving Cream

Directions:

This was invented by one of our teachers while messing around with the stuff. I was attempting to clean up at the end of Summer Session in 2008. We had a big tub of ooblick left over from the workshop and he asked what would happen if we added shaving cream to it. And, since I had no idea what would happen, I said TRY IT AND SEE!

It was like creamy ooblick. I know you want to know how much cream he used. He used lots. Try it out yourself and let me know what you think.

Small Motor Skills

Math/Counting

Estimating

Social Skills

Opposites (wet/dry)

Evaporation

Physical Changes

Chemical Reactions

Dramatic Play

Language Development

Sensory Awareness

Use of Tools

WHIP IT UP!

Although Ivory® Snow Flakes have been discontinued, you can make them yourself by grating bars of Ivory® Soap. Remember too that Ivory® is soooo soft that you can "grate it" with a popsicle stick! I suggest having the children do the grating.

You Need: 5-10 Bars of Ivory® Soap
Hand held egg beaters
Water
A way to grate the soap (cheese grater or popsicle sticks)

Directions:
Have the children grate about 5-10 bars of soap. Put the grated soap in the sensory tub and add enough warm water to cover the soap. Provide manual egg beaters and let the children whip it up and beat those bubbles!

From the Ooey Gooey® Test Kitchens:
We found that you can even "grate" the soap just by scraping your fingernails over it. Also, it doesn't have to be Ivory® soap, but it has to be a brand of soap that is soft. We found Dove® and Ivory® to work the best.

Small Motor Skills

Math/Measurement

Counting

Physical and Chemical Changes

Social Skills

Dramatic Play

Language Development

Sensory Awareness

Use of Tools

JELLY CAKE

Small Motor Skills

Math/Measurement

Counting

Color Mixing

Social Skills

Dramatic Play

Language Development

Sensory Awareness

Use of Tools

This one was invented by a child who attended one of our Playdays in the Park while we were still living in San Diego. During a moment of exploration (when I guess he thought no one was watching) he took a Knox® Mold from the Knox® Table and dumped it into a sensory tub filled with shaving cream. He started squishing the Knox® and the Cream together while yelling to the air, "Look at me! Look at me! I am making a jelly cake!"

I am not sure where he conjured up the name nor do I know what moved him to mix it. But I am glad he felt the freedom to do so. It has become one of the best things we do.

You Need: Knox® Molds of various shapes and sizes. (See page 160)
Shaving Cream
Food Coloring or Liquid Water Color

Directions:
Put the Knox® Molds in your sensory tub Cover the tops of them with shaving cream. Drip drop some coloring on the cream.

Break it apart with hands, mix together, add more color and cream as necessary. It takes on the appearance of Ambrosia Salad. It really is an amazing texture.

From the Ooey Gooey® Test Kitchens:
You can hold clear colored chunks of Knox® up to a window and see the light and colors coming through.

Reality Check:
Not everyone cares though so don't be upset if you are the only one who thinks it's pretty.

WASHING BABIES

This one is pretty basic but will often become a fast favorite.

You Need: Waterproof baby dolls
Soapy water
Towels
Sponges
Bath puffs

Directions:
Wash baby dolls in the sensory tub. Have towels available so the children can dry their babies.

Suggestion:
I place the baby dolls in a basket or bin next to the soapy water filled sensory tub. This way the children get to pick which baby they want to wash.

From the Ooey Gooey® Test Kitchens:
We decided that we like the *Lots To Love*® brand of baby dolls because they are entirely washable and waterproof.

Small Motor Skills

Math/Measurement

Counting

Opposites (wet/dry)

Social Skills

Dramatic Play

Language Development

Sensory Awareness

Use of Tools

GLUE AND SHAVING CREAM

You Need: Glue

Shaving Cream

(optional) Food Coloring or Liquid Water Color

Directions:

Mix together (roughly) equal parts of shaving cream and glue.

But remember that like many of our favorite sensory tub activities there is no right or wrong way to make it. If you use more cream, it will feel fluffier. If you use more glue it will be heavier, thicker and stickier.

Continue to play with the formula until you find one you like the best.

This is good for tactile exploration, squeezing and stirring. One guy played with it for so long it made glue strings between his fingers. It looked liked webs. He held up his webby hands and said, "Hey look! I made a web site!" Clever!

Small Motor Skills

Math/Measurement

Counting

Physical and Chemical Changes

Social Skills

Dramatic Play

Language Development

Sensory Awareness

Use of Tools

TIN CAN GOGGLES

Small Motor Skills

Math/Measurement

Opposites (wet/dry)

Evaporation

Counting

Social Skills

Dramatic Play

Language Development

Sensory Awareness

Use of Tools

You Need: An assortment of cylindrical shaped cans and bottles
Plastic wrap (like Saran Wrap®)
Rubber bands
Masking tape or duct tape for the edges of the cans

Directions:

To make tin can goggles you need a collection of large cans, water bottles and soda bottles all with the tops and bottoms cut off. Put masking tape or duct tape around the edges of the can so they are not as sharp. Secure a piece of plastic wrap over one end of your tin can goggle with a rubberband.

The children can then look through their goggles into the water table and see what is going on under the surface.

FLOUR AND BABY OIL

You Need: 1 bag of flour (5 lbs.)

3-5 bottles of baby oil (any brand)

Start with this ratio and adjust as necessary based on the size of your sensory tub and your preferred consistency of this creamy mixture.

Directions:

Dump the full bag of flour into your sensory tub. You are going to add the baby oil one bottle at a time until you obtain the consistency you and the children like best. It ends up looking like cookie dough. Add a little bit more oil and it will look like runny cookie dough. Some prefer it thick and almost "moldable" some like it a bit goopier. Let the children decide.

From the Ooey Gooey® Test Kitchens:

We unanimously decided this should be on the "menu" at every day spa in the country.

Small Motor Skills

Math/Measurement

Counting

Social Skills

Dramatic Play

Language Development

Sensory Awareness

Use of Tools

AQUARIUM GRAVEL

You Need: Aquarium Gravel (Find it at a pet store)

Directions:
Put multicolored aquarium gravel in your sensory tub for scooping and pouring.

For the Adventurous:
Do you have decorations from an old aquarium laying around? Did you get some at a garage sale? Acquire them in a move? What about turning your sensory tub into a (fish optional) aquarium! The colored gravel, some rock formations, maybe some of the decorations and some water. Check that out!

Small Motor Skills (holding, pouring, scooping)

Volume

Measurement

Estimating

Social Skills

Opposites (hard/soft)

Dramatic Play

Language Development

Sensory Awareness

Use of Tools

COCOA MULCH

Cocoa Mulch is made from the shells of a cocoa bean and is a great
sensory experience. It smells great (like chocolate!) and feels crunchy.
You can get it from various home and garden stores or from www.kodokids.com.

Provide it in the sensory tub for scooping and pouring.

Small Motor Skills

Math/Measurement

Counting

Social Skills

Dramatic Play

Language Development

Sensory Awareness

Use of Tools

CORKS AND CORNMEAL

Important Note Before Starting:
Make sure to always add a good amount of salt to your sensory tub cornmeal. Otherwise you will grow (grow? Or is it get?) mealy-worms. Gross.

Small Motor Skills

Volume

Measurement

Estimating

Social Skills

Opposites (hard/soft)

Dramatic Play

Language Development

Sensory Awareness

Use of Tools

You Need: Cornmeal
Salt
Corks

Directions:
Put the cornmeal (and salt) in the sensory tub with a bunch of corks. Nothing too tricky or "special" with this one here, but for some reason this combination was always a big hit. They would scoop the cornmeal, stack the corks, make designs with the corks, pour the cornmeal over the corks....

From the Ooey Gooey® Test Kitchens:
Our testers loved having to accumulate corks for this particular activity, "Open another bottle! It's for the children!" But seriously, for the few (and I do say few) of you who possibly don't generate enough corks on your own (ahem) you can purchase them at craft stores, or call a local winery, or, for you brave ones, schedule a wine tasting trip and write it all off as a business expense! Have Fun!

FEED CORN AND CORN HUSKERS

Ideally you will obtain a couple corn huskers and some feed corn still on the cob. The children can put the ear of feed corn in the husker, turn the crank and watch the husker pull the kernels off the cob. The kernels fall into the sensory tub and the cob shoots out the side. Great fun!

You can then put the cobs back in the tub with the corn, or you can paint with them, or add them to your compost heap. I watched adults play with a corn husker for 30 minutes straight. There is something amazing about turning that crank and watching the cob shoot out the side!

I am well aware of budgetary considerations. I know that for many of you this activity will require a financial investment of some kind. I urge you to be creative. Ask parents, get on E-bay, meet a local farmer, do a fundraiser. Or you might decide to just make the purchase yourself. The effort and investment will be worth it. I guarantee that at some point you will want this equipment for your program.

Small Motor Skills

Math/Measurement

Counting

Social Skills

Dramatic Play

Language Development

Sensory Awareness

Use of Tools

Some Basics:
A 50 lb. bag of feed corn will yield about 100 ears of corn and will cost anywhere from $15 - $25. Check online, your local feed store or a local farmers market for the best deal near you.

A new manual **corn husker** sells for about $150 - $200. We found used ones on E-bay anywhere from $10 - $200. But as always, Caveat Emptor! Buyer Beware! Be sure to inquire as to whether or not they work before buying all the $10 ones and thinking you got such a great deal!

FLOUR, CORNMEAL, SALT AND POPCORN

One of our favorite anti-recipe recipes. By anti-recipe I mean there is no right or wrong ratio or mixture.

Small Motor Skills

Math/Measurement

Counting

Social Skills

Dramatic Play

Language Development

Sensory Awareness

Use of Tools

In your sensory tub mix together in any amount or ratio:
> Flour
> Cornmeal
> Salt (only being added to kept the mealy-worms away,
>> so you don't need that much)
> Unpopped popcorn kernels

Reality Check:
Someone is going to pick out all the kernels. Have small little cups or containers available.

TREASURE SAND

Put some regular **Play Sand** in your sensory tub. Some children have not ever played with plain sand. Don't be in a hurry to sexy it up. Sometimes basic is best. When interest is waning you can bury things in the dry sand. Some of my favorites:

- Rocks that I have spray painted gold
- Those flat, glass marbles used in the bottom of flower vases
- Sea shells
- Plain rocks

Variations:

You can dampen the sand with squirt bottles or misters.
Try adding cars, trucks or even some small animals to the sand too.

Small Motor Skills

Math/Measurement

Counting

Social Skills

Dramatic Play

Language Development

Sensory Awareness

Use of Tools

75

MAGNIFICENT MAGNETICS

Small Motor Skills

Math/Measurement

Science/Magnetics

Counting

Social Skills

Dramatic Play

Language Development

Sensory Awareness

Use of Tools

Directions:

Add small magnetic objects (magnetic balls & chips, actual magnets, paper clips, bottle caps, metal Hot Wheels™ , etc.) to any dry sensory tub material (sand, dirt, cornmeal, rice, etc). Provide magnetic wands and go on a magnet hunt in your sensory tub.

After doing it a couple times add things that are NOT magnetic.

Play with adding new magnetic and non-magnetic items to the dry sensory tub material. Are some of the children becoming curious? Maybe this will springboard into a magnetic vs. non-magnetic investigation in your classroom.

Be ready to do some list making, charting and graphing!

CINNAMON OATS

Double this if you have a large sensory tub!

You Need: 1 big container (42 oz.) of uncooked Oats
1 cup salt
½ cup cinnamon (adjust as needed based on
how "smelly" you want it!)

Directions:
Stir. Mix. Play. Great smells will fill your classroom.

Small Motor Skills
Math/Measurement
Counting
Social Skills
Dramatic Play
Language Development
Sensory Awareness
Use of Tools

FLOUR AND COLORED RICE

Small Motor Skills

Math/Measurement

Counting

Social Skills

Dramatic Play

Language Development

Sensory Awareness

Use of Tools

Mix together flour and colored rice.
You make Colored Rice the same way you make colored pasta (See pages 80/81).

Many of you know the story of my little guy who spent all day using tweezers to remove all of the blue rice.   So much for supposedly not having a long attention span!

Variation:
Try Flour, Glitter and Sequins in the sensory tub.

Another Variation:
Try Salt, Glitter and Sequins in the sensory tub.

From the Ooey Gooey® Test Kitchens:
We found that flour can make the surrounding floor area a bit slick. Take precaution and be sure you have a sheet or drop cloth positioned under the sensory tub when you use flour in your sensory tubs.

COLORED ROCK SALT

You Need: Rock Salt (in the baking aisle)
Liquid Water Color or food coloring

Directions:
Color a few bags of rock salt. Put it in the sensory tub for exploration. Color the rock salt the same way you would color pasta (See pages 80/81).

One time when we made this, the chunks of rock salt in the bag were just huge! I am not sure if we just got a "good bag" or what! This mixture stayed out in the tub for about a week. We added shovels, spoons and magnifying glasses. One of the children excitedly announced that he had found "precious, precious jewels!"

Small Motor Skills
Math/Measurement
Counting
Social Skills
Dramatic Play
Language Development
Sensory Awareness
Use of Tools

COLORED DRY PASTA

Small Motor Skills

Math/Measurement

Counting

Sorting

Color Recognition

Social Skills

Dramatic Play

Language Development

Sensory Awareness

Use of Tools

Colored dry pasta is a good thing to have around. It can be used as a dry material in your sensory tubs for scooping and pouring, for collage art gluing and even for stringing necklaces. Try different kinds of pasta noodles such as penne, macaroni elbows, shells, etc.

If you use *liquid watercolor* to color the pasta it will dry immediately and you will not have to use rubbing alcohol. If you use *food coloring* you will need to mix TONS of food coloring with rubbing alcohol in order to color the pasta and you will have to spread it out on newspaper so it will dry overnight.

Directions:

Separate the dry pasta into bowls. Squirt it with liquid water color. Stir. Add more color until it reaches your desired pigment. By the time you finish coloring, squirting and stirring your pasta will be dry and ready for use! If you store your dry, colored pasta in an airtight container it will keep indefinitely.

There are hundreds of kinds of pasta to choose from. My favorites to color for the sensory tub include:

- Wagon Wheels (Rotelle)
- Penne
- Rigatoni
- Elbow Macaroni
- Small Shells
- Bow Ties (Farfalle)
- Spirals (Fusilli)

Suggestion:

Make colored rice the same way as outlined here.

GROWING GRASS

This is pretty straight forward. You can grow grass in your sensory tub, or in a small shallow plastic container or even in egg cartons.

You Need: Potting soil
Grass seeds
Something to grow the grass in

Directions:
Put the soil in the bottom of the sensory tub (or whatever you are using to grow the grass in). Sprinkle grass seeds on the top. Water daily. Once the grass has started growing you can cut it with scissors.

Suggestion:
Some children will naturally get into comparing and contrasting and estimating by having various containers around the room. One with lots of sunlight, one with none, one in the cupboard, one with lots of water, too much water, not enough water, etc. Lots of science experimentation, observation and documentation will occur with this simple activity.

From the Ooey Gooey® Test Kitchens:
Our favorite way of growing the grass was in Styrofoam egg cartons!

Small Motor Skills

Math/Measurement

Graphing and Charting

Opposites (wet/dry)

Evaporation

Estimating

Social Skills

Physical Changes

Dramatic Play

Language Development

Sensory Awareness

Use of Tools

FLAX SEED

Flax Seed seems to be easier to find than ever before. I will suggest NOT buying it from your health food store as it is sold in too small of a quantity and you will pay a fortune. Look for it in bulk at your local feed store, check your local yellow pages, or of course, check online.

Directions:
Play with dry flax seed in the sensory tub.

Then as the children continue exploring the feeling and texture, add some warm water. Oh my goodness. If you have not felt this before you are just going to love it. To me it feels like molasses. When you add the water to the dry seed, the oil from the seed is released and the mixture almost feels like syrup. Have a wash-hands bucket close by.

Small Motor Skills

Math/Measurement

Counting

Social Skills

Dramatic Play

Language Development

Sensory Awareness

Use of Tools

Clean Up Advice:
Clean up on this one can be a bit time consuming but DO NOT let that deter you from exploring the mixture. The real trick is to keep it damp enough so that it sticks to itself and not to your sensory tub. If it dries out too much after being wet it will stick like glue and seems to not come off the sides of the tub.

We kept it for about 2 days and then it started to sprout and grow! Which was a neat project in and of itself, but if you are looking for sensory and tactile and not necessarily a new garden, this one has about a 2 day window of exploration before it takes on a new look!

SENSORY WALK

Large Motor Skills

Math/Counting

Social Skills

Opposites (wet/dry)

Language Development

Sensory Awareness

Directions:

In smaller dish pan style sensory tubs try putting some of these suggestions on the ground and facilitate a sensory walk:

- Ice cube trays with interesting shapes
- Water (warm and/or cold)
- Sand (wet and/or dry)
- Sandpaper (tape a couple strips to the bottom of the sensory tub)
- Cotton
- Silk Squares
- Foam/Packing Peanuts
- Flax Seed
- Floam (see page 48)
- Flour
- Mud
- Cornmeal
- Rice
- Cooked Spaghetti
- Unpopped popcorn kernels
- Carpet Squares
- Ooblick   (page 59)

Don't put out too many sensations at once. That can be overwhelming! I would start with 3 or 4 and build on that. Be sure to have a "wash foot bucket" set up for the children to wash off when they are done.

Some children who will NOT touch with their hands will touch with their feet. And remember too that just because Emma enjoys playing in the ooblick with her hands, that does not guarantee that she will enjoy how it feels on her feet!

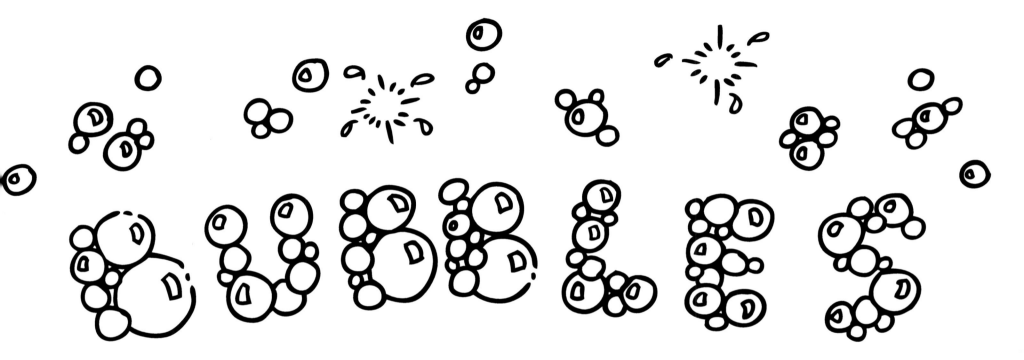

BASIC BUBBLES

You Need: 6 cups water
2 cups Dawn®

Basic Bubbles *plus 1*
6 cups water
2 cups Dawn®
2 TBS glycerin (available at most drug stores for about $4)

Basic Bubbles *plus 2*
6 cups water
2 cups Dawn®
2 TBS glycerin (available at most drug stores for about $4)
½ cup Mr. Bubble® bubble bath

Chemical Reactions

Surface Tension

Air/Wind

Problem Solving

Scientific Inquiry Skills ("Why?")

Counting

Use of Tools

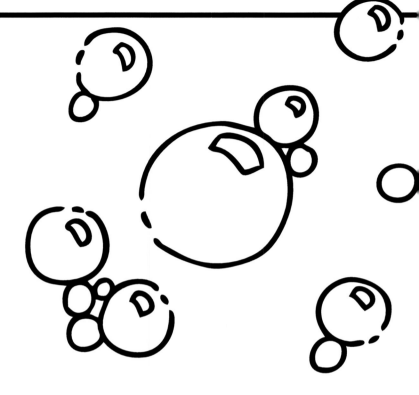

BUBBLE MIXTURE II - THE REMIX

You Need: 12 cups water
1 cup either Joy® or Dawn® dish soap (we used Dawn® in our tests)
1 cup cornstarch
2 TBS baking powder

Chemical Reactions
Surface Tension
Air/Wind
Problem Solving
Scientific Inquiry Skills ("Why?")
Counting
Use of Tools

Try this recipe when making your next batch of bubbles. We found it to be more forgiving – meaning, the bubbles seemed to withstand more poking and prodding from little fingers. And the bubbles seemed to last a little longer in the air and on our hands and on the table. The mixture seemed to not be as sticky or as soapy as when we just mixed dish soap and water. Try it out.

The cornstarch will settle at the bottom in between uses, so be ready to reconstitute it before blowing bubbles.

FOAMY BUBBLE "SNAKES" #1
MADE WITH: PVC PIPE AND CHEESECLOTH

You Need: 8-inch pieces of PVC pipe
Small Rubberbands
Cheesecloth
Sandpaper (optional)

Directions:

Most of these materials can be found at your local hardware or home improvement store. The little rubberbands can be found at most drug stores.

PVC pipe comes in 10 ft. sections at a hardware store. 10-ft of pipe will make 15 (fifteen), 8-inch pieces. If you ask them nicely (and if the store is not too busy) they might cut the pipe into the pieces for you. If not, you will need to use either a hack saw or a PVC cutter and do it yourself.

So now you have 15 pieces of PVC pipe measuring 8-inches each.
Use the sandpaper to smooth the ends of the pipe if they are too rough.

Chemical Reactions

Surface Tension

Air/Wind

Problem Solving

Scientific Inquiry Skills ("Why?")

Counting

Use of Tools

Math/Measurement

Cut the cheesecloth into 15, 2-inch x 1-inch rectangles. Fold the rectangles in half to make 1-inch squares. Use a rubberband to attach a square of cheesecloth to one end of each PVC pipe. Now you have a PVC pipe bubble blower!

From the Ooey Gooey® Test Kitchens:
If you use a true PVC Cutter to cut the pipe, the edges will typically be smooth and will not require much smoothing out with sandpaper. If you use a hacksaw you will definitely need to sand the edges to make them smoother!

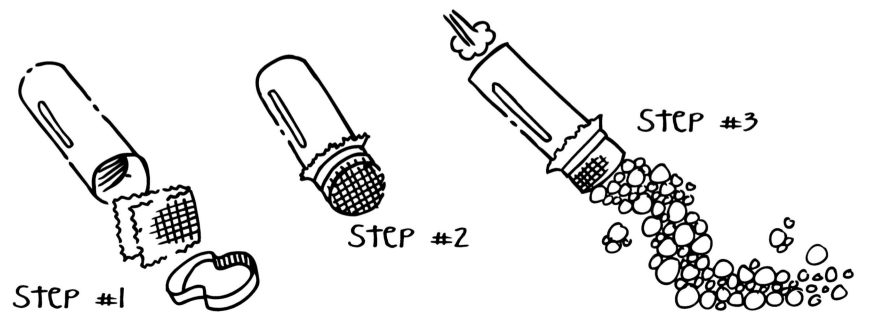

STep #3

STep #2

STep #1

FOAMY BUBBLE "SNAKES" #2
MADE WITH: NYLONS AND TP TUBES

Chemical Reactions

Surface Tension

Air/Wind

Problem Solving

Scientific Inquiry Skills ("Why?")

Counting

Use of Tools

Math/Measurement

You Need: Squares of nylon stockings
Paper towel and/or toilet paper tubes
Rubberbands

Directions:
You will pretty much make a contraption that is similar to the PVC pipe blower, but you will use squares of nylons and toilet paper tubes (or paper towel tubes).

Where as the PVC pipe blowers are sturdier, durable and last forever, these are more disposable and typically can be made at a moments notice.

FOAMY BUBBLE "SNAKES" #3
MADE WITH: WATER BOTTLES AND AN OLD TOWEL

You Need: Water bottle
X-ACTO® knife
Rubber band
Washcloth or old towel you can cut up

Chemical Reactions

Surface Tension

Air/Wind

Problem Solving

Scientific Inquiry Skills ("Why?")

Counting

Use of Tools

Math/Measurement

Directions:

Again, same idea as the other two. Use the X-ACTO®
knife to carefully cut the bottom off a water bottle.
Cut a square of cloth/towel that fits over the hole.
Attach it to the bottom of the bottle with a rubber band.

SHREDDED PAPER AND LIQUID STARCH

You Need: Shredded paper (collected from the shredder in someone's office)
Liquid Starch
A place to dry your creations
Patience (it takes a couple days for them to dry)

Creativity

Small Motor Skills

Physical Characteristics

Opposites (wet/dry)

Evaporation

Descriptive Language

Dramatic Play and Imagination

Directions:

There is no real recipe for this one. The idea is that you are going to mix the paper and starch together, squeeze out the extra starch and mold it into various shapes. You can make them as big or as small as you want. Let them dry completely before using them in the classroom.

Variations:

Maybe they will be bricks in the building/block area. Or maybe they will be "boulders" at the Dinosaur table. Or maybe you will weigh them on the scale in the science center....

Suggestions:

Allow the children to mold whatever shapes they want. However you can use pre-shaped molds, like cookie cutters to make hearts, etc. or cut a ½ gallon paper milk carton in half and make brick shapes, etc. The only limit is your imagination! I would suggest though that you permit and encourage free-form modeling and exploration before getting all crazy about making "things" or "shapes". Allow that to come from the children. Beware of too much adult direction with open ended activities.

SHAVING CREAM AND GLUE PAINT

You Need: A mixture of shaving cream and glue
Paper

Directions:
Shaving cream and glue is one of our favorite mixtures for the sensory tub (See page 65). We also have been known to paint with it. So mix up a good sized batch of glue and shaving cream, plop some down on paper and have fun painting with fingers, brushes or maybe even your elbow!

Variations:
Forget the paper and just plop it right down on the table and make a table top mural. Clean it off with a squeegee.

From the Ooey Gooey® Test Kitchens:
We found that when it dries on the paper, it gets stiff and puffs up a little. Kind of like little mountains.

Creativity

Self Expression

Small Motor

Scribbling

Color Mixing

Painting

Descriptive Language

Sensory Awareness

GLUE PROJECT IN TWO PARTS

You Need: Glue
Construction Paper
Two Days

Creativity

Small Motor Skills

Painting and Design

Descriptive Language

Part I Directions:

Squeeze glue randomly all over your paper. Just make a gluey design. Let it dry completely. You can use clear or colored glue and any kind of paper.

Part II Directions:

After it has dried all the way, paint, color, chalk, inside, around, over the glue designs.

PATCHWORKS COLLAGE

You Need: Fabric samples or scraps
Upholstery sample books
Cardboard
Glue

Directions:

Make a patchwork collage from the various fabric samples and textures and glue onto sturdy paper or cardboard.

Creativity
Small Motor Skills
Shape Recognition
Math/Counting
Color and Number Recognition
Descriptive Language
Spatial Skills
Texture
Sensory Awareness

COLORED GLUE AND POPSICLE STICKS

You Need: Colored Glue
Paper
Popsicle Sticks

I saw this when I walked into the Toddler Room awhile back. The teacher has put a big sheet of butcher paper on the table along with an assortment of small cups filled with colored glue. The children were squiggling the glue all over the paper with popsicle sticks!

Tip:
Make your own colored glue by adding food coloring or Liquid Watercolor to the glue you already have on hand.

Variation:
Use wax paper instead of regular art paper

From the Ooey Gooey® Test Kitchens:
We found this to be a good way for children to still get to use glue without squeezing $10 worth of it all over the paper.

Creativity
Self Expression
Color Recognition
Problem Solving
Social Skills
Use of Tools

COLLAGE ART

You Need: Paper
Collage Items
Glue

Directions:
Have fun making collage designs with glue and your collection of (preferably recycled) materials!

Creativity
Small Motor Skills
Math/Counting
Descriptive Language
Spatial Skills
Texture
Sensory Awareness

A few of my favorite collage items:
- Cut up pieces of wallpaper samples
- Corks
- Paper scraps
- Water bottle lids
- Bottle caps
- Buttons
- Cotton balls
- String
- TP tubes cut into sections
- Larger beads
- Cut pieces of curling ribbon
- Glitter
- The lids to dried-out markers
- Popsicle sticks

Provide a basket of collage materials for the children to choose from. Provide sturdy paper or paper plates for the collages to be built on. Regular paper can be kind of flimsy, but it does work. If using regular art paper, place a section of newspaper under the paper they are working on so you can lift it up and move it easily to the place where it will be allowed to dry.

3-D BOX ART CANVAS

You Need: Various sizes and shapes of recycled, empty and clean, paper boxes and containers. Such as: oatmeal containers, cereal boxes, food stuffs like Pop-Tarts®, Granola boxes, etc.

Directions:

First you need to get the boxes on the wall. Depending on the space and the flexibility of the powers that be, you can either tape or staple them.

If attaching the boxes to the wall is not an option, then make 3-D Tower Canvases in the block center instead. Build a structure or tower with your boxes and glue (try Gorilla® Super Glue) or duct tape it together. Paint it after it is dry.

Tips:

If doing it from the wall, be sure to attach the containers at the child's level. Add some liquid starch or glue to your paint to keep it from flaking when painting your creations.

Variation:

You can wrap the boxes in paper before using them. This gives the visual impression of a blank canvas and also serves to cover up the commercial and/or product images.

Construction

Elements of Design

Spatial Awareness

Large Motor Skills

Math/Counting

Descriptive Language

Creativity

Cooperation and Social Skills

Estimating

Gravity

3-D Construction

106

GLITTERY YARN BALLS

You Need: Balloons
Glue
Yarn
Glitter

Directions:

Blow up a small balloon for each child. Soak the yarn in a mixture of glue and water. (Liquid Starch will work if you have that on hand). Assist the children in wrapping the gluey string all the way around the balloon. This process takes a little bit of dexterity and a whole lot of patience. While still wet and sticky, shake glitter all over the balloon. Let it dry. Once dry, pop the balloon and remove the pieces of popped balloon.

Suggestion:

Hang these festive balls around the room!

1. Decorate it.   2. Pop it.   3. Hang it.

SODA BOTTLE FLOWERS

You Need: Paint
Paper
Recycled water bottles

Directions:

Make prints on paper with the bottoms of water bottles. I especially like the Aquafina® brand because the bottoms look like the petals of a flower.

Creativity

Self Expression

Painting

Color Mixing

Elements of Design

Spatial Awareness

Small Motor Skills

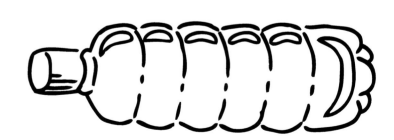

110

TROLL DOLL PAINTING

You Need: Troll Dolls

Paint

Paper

Directions:

Paint with troll dolls! You can use their funky hair as a brush or make prints with their feet. What else can you find around the house to paint with?

Creativity

Self Expression

Painting

Color Mixing

Elements of Design

Spatial Awareness

Small Motor Skills

TOE PAINTING

Creativity

Self Expression

Painting

Color Mixing

Elements of Design

Spatial Awareness

Small Motor Skills

Large Motor Skills

Sensory Awareness

Yes we all love feet-painting and making foot prints. But this is a little different. Check it out:

Hold the paint brush with your toes. Paint a picture with your foot instead of your hand.

Reality Check:
This could (and might!) turn into foot painting. Be ready with some towels and water for washing.

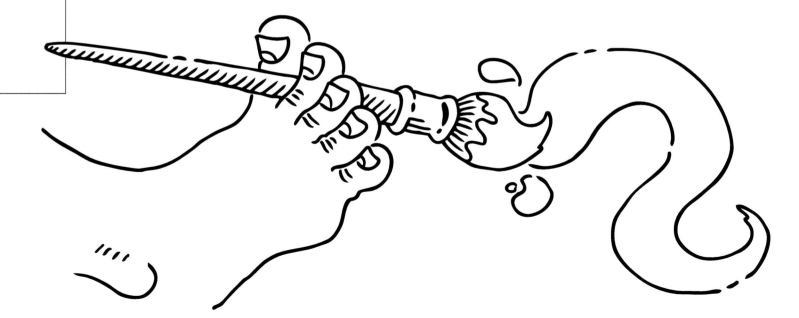

FOOT PAINTING: SIDEWAYS STYLE
"WHAT!?" YOU ASK. YOU ARE GOING TO LOVE THIS.

You Need: Butcher Paper
Tape
Paint
Wash Foot Bucket
Towels to dry feet after washing

Large Motor Skills
Spatial Awareness
Body Awareness
Creativity
Socialization Skills
Language Development
Color Mixing

Directions:

Tape a large piece of butcher paper to the lower half of the wall. The children

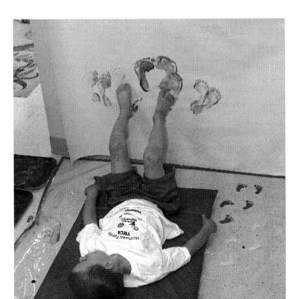

will lay down on the floor and paint the paper with their feet *while they are on their backs*.

A wild idea! You might want to try it at your next dinner party. Maybe.

BIG SHOE PRINTS

Creativity

Self Expression

Painting

Color Mixing

Elements of Design

Spatial Awareness

Small Motor Skills

Large Motor Skills/Balance

Cooperation

Color Mixing

Use of Tools

You Need: An assortment of adult sized shoes

Butcher paper

Paper

A shallow tray of paint

Directions:

Tape the paper down to the floor or driveway. Children can choose the "dress up" shoes they want to wear. Step carefully into the shallow tray of paint and walk the runway in their fancy shoes!

From the Ooey Gooey® Test Kitchens:

The children just Love! Love! Love! to wear Mr. Tom's big sneakers when doing this painting project!

CORN COB PRINTING

You Need: Paint
Paper
Corn cobs

Directions:

You can make artistic designs with corn cobs. Roll them on the paper, stamp the ends of paper, use cobs with kernels, cobs without kernels. Use regular corn, feed corn, multi-colored corn or even realistic-looking (but fake) corn cobs from craft stores... Go corn crazy!

CRAYON RESIST

You Need: Crayola® Crayons (they do work the best for this one)
Thin, thin, thin watered down black paint (tempra or liquid water color)
Paper
Brushes

Creativity

Self Expression

Small Motor Skills

Scribbling

Painting

Descriptive Language

Directions:
This activity has two parts:
1) color all over the paper with the crayons and then...
2) apply a layer of the watered down black paint over the crayon designs.
The wax resists the water so the crayon shows through. The harder they press and the thicker their designs the more dramatic the "resist" effect will be.

Variation:
Use white crayons on white paper. Then observe the contrast of black (paint) and white (crayons). You can actually thin down ANY color of paint to go over the crayons. The darker colors of course will have the most dramatic effect. I have used construction paper, copy paper and regular art paper for this one. They all work.

STRING PULL ART

You Need: String
Paper
Paint

Directions:
String pulling is pretty much the same as Fold Over Blottos (page 118/119) except before folding the paper over you will drop a long piece of string into the paint. A section of the string needs to be sticking out the side of the paper after you fold it over. Why? Because after you fold the paper over, you will pull the string and ZIP! Open the paper and look at your design!

The larger the paper the more dramatic the string pulling effect.

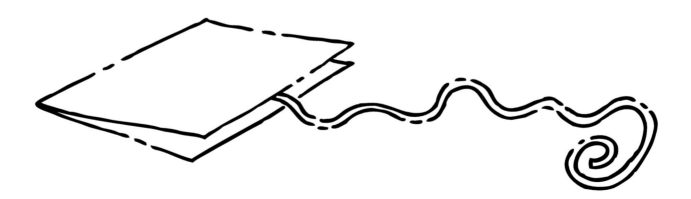

BLOTTO PRINTS
(ALSO CALLED "FOLD OVER PRINTS")

I like "Blotto" better. It's fun to say.

You Need: Paper (folded in half)
Paint

Creativity

Self Expression

Small Motor Skills

Painting

Symmetry

Printmaking

Elements of Design

Descriptive Language

Directions:
You can pre-fold the paper to make it easier for smaller hands. Put a spoonful of paint on the paper. Fold the paper over. Smooth the paper with your hand. Open your paper back up and see the same print on the other side of the paper. Try it with one color of paint, try it with two. Shoot! Try it with three!

Suggestion:
Many teachers combine this activity with the book *It Looked Like Spilt Milk* by Charles Shaw. When they do, they typically provide blue construction paper and white paint to replicate the illustrations in the book. That is fine. Remember though that it is OK to do this art separate from the book as well. Don't "save" this project only for when you read *It Looked Like Spilt Milk*.

A few ways to get the paint on the paper:

Brushes

Fingers

Squeeze bottles

Spoons

You can also play with the consistency of the paint.

Tip:

The children who get into this activity get into it BIG TIME and they will want to make tons and tons of prints. Be aware of this fact *before* setting out this activity so you can avoid "Everyone gets to make *one*!" syndrome. Someone *will* need to make 10. Be ready and be prepared.

MASKING TAPE LIFT OFF

This one takes a little more fine motor coordination.

Creativity

Self Expression

Small Motor Skills

Painting

Descriptive Language

You Need: Masking Tape
Paper
Paint

Directions:
Essentially you will place pieces of masking tape all over the paper, paint over the tape and then pull the tape off.

Reality Check:
Many children will just want to paint over the tape and really don't care about lifting the tape up. Remember to be flexible.

SMELLY PAINTS

Time to raid the spice rack! Add spices, scents, extracts or even essential oils to your tempra paint when doing any painting project.

Favorite smells:
- Almond
- Vanilla
- Coffee grounds
- Mint
- Cinnamon
- Nutmeg
- Lavender
- Sage
- Thyme

Creativity

Painting

Self Expression

Small Motor Skills

Sensory Discrimination

Sensory Awareness

Descriptive Language

Use of Tools

EASY BREEZY FINGER PAINT

You Need: Liquid Starch
Tempra paint
A squirt of dish soap

Essentially you are adding a little bit of dish soap and a little bit of liquid starch to the tempra paint you already have on hand. The dish soap will ease in hand-washing. The liquid starch thins the tempra without watering it down too much, helps the picture dry and assists in keeping the paint adhered to the paper.

Directions:

Fill the paint cup ½ full with tempra paint.

Pour in a little bit of liquid starch.

Then squirt in some dish soap.

Mix with a spoon and then use that same spoon to scoop the paint onto the paper for a fingerpainting exploration.

Creativity

Self Expression

Small Motor Skills

Color Mixing

Painting

Descriptive Language

Sensory Awareness

SQUEEZE DESIGNS
-OR-
CONDIMENT CREATIVITY

You Need: Tempra Paint in recycled squeezable bottles

Directions:

For extra fun put yellow paint in a mustard bottle, red paint in a catsup bottle and white paint in a mayonnaise bottle. Put paint in various squeeze bottles and watch the creativity fly. Some will end up fingerpainting, some will fold their papers, some will just squeeze....

Creativity
Small Motor Skills
Color Mixing
Painting and Design
Descriptive Language
Sensory Awareness

WADS OF NEWSPAPER DESIGNS

Creativity

Self Expression

Small Motor Skills

Color Mixing

Painting

Descriptive Language

Sensory Awareness

You Need: Big sheets of paper

Paint

Wads of newspaper

Directions:

This one is pretty straight forward. Scrunch up a piece of newspaper, hold it in your hand and paint with it.

From the Ooey Gooey® Test Kitchens:

We tried it on the easel, and then on paper taped to the wall, and to the floor.

HAT PAINTING

You Need: Baseball Caps
Visors
Construction Helmets
Duct Tape
Paint Brushes
Paint

Creativity

Painting

Spatial Skills

Cooperation and Working Together

Tracking

Use of Tools

Directions:
Duct tape a paint brush to the brims of the hats and helmets. Use these unique painting tools to paint at the easel or to make a mural on paper you have taped to the wall.

Suggestion:
Paint at the easel, on a big piece of paper taped to a wall, or even your sliding glass door (just hose it off when you are done!)

STOMPER PRINTS

Remember playing with these as a kid?

You Need: Romper Stompers
Paper
Paint

Balance

Large Motor Skills

Creativity

Shape Recognition

Painting

Print Making

Color Mixing

Directions:

Wear your Romper Stompers through a little bit of paint and then walk on
your paper.

You can purchase commercially made Romper Stompers or you
can make them with tin cans and string.

PAPER BAG PARTY HATS

Creativity

Small Motor Skills

Bubbles/Surface Tension

Air/Blowing

Math/Counting

Shapes and Colors

Descriptive Language

You Need: At least one big brown paper grocery bag for each child

Paint

Brushes or other objects to paint with

Or you can go the collage, glitter and glue route for decorating…

You know them best!

Directions:

There are two ways to do this depending on the ages, dexterity (and patience) of the children.

Decorate first, roll *later*.

Roll first, decorate *now*.

With younger children I will bring the hats to school all ready rolled up so they can jump right into decorating them.

Here's how to roll the bag hats:

Completely open the bag.

Carefully start rolling the edges down and around. Keep rolling until the hat opening is small enough (or large enough!) to fit on their head.

Reality Check:

Someone will paint inside the hat, someone won't paint it at all, someone will paint it so much that it will be too heavy to wear as a hat. Someone will turn it into a basket and won't even want a hat. Someone won't want anything to do with the "stoopid poopy hats" in the first place. You know what I mean. Leave it alone and don't push it.

STRINGING NECKLACES

Stringing beads and noodles is another great activity. I have found that even in the absence of adult prompting children will want to wear their stringing as a "necklace."

Hand-Eye Coordination

Small Motor Skills

Creativity

Cooking Skills

Math/Counting

Social Skills

Language Development

Following Directions

Dramatic Play

You Need: String

Masking tape

Things to string:
Straw pieces, colored pastas, 1-inch squares of paper with holes punched in the center and/or beads (ones you have made from clay or store bought).

Directions:
Set out the choices of things to string in containers. Allow the children to choose the pattern and design of their stringing.

Suggestion:

Tape the end of the string on top of the table so their materials do not slide off the end. Put their initials or name on the tape if necessary. Let them string. Some will fill the entire string with various materials, some will only use one or two things. That's OK.

Variation:

Partner Stringing

Follow the same procedure above except cut a longer piece of string and tape the middle of the string to the table. Two children will work cooperatively at the same time, each stringing from one end of the string to the center.

3-D CURLEY-Q PAPER STRIP ART

This one can be a bit of a challenge for smaller hands. It takes a little more direction than many of the other activities presented here for you. Some years the kids just love this and others they just don't. Don't push it.

Creativity

Small Motor Skills

Spatial Skills

3-D Designs

Elements of Design

Construction

Cooperation

Directions:

Adult's job the day or night before: Start with sheets of different colored construction paper. Start cutting the paper (in no particular order) vertically and horizontally. This will give you various sizes and lengths of colored paper strips.

The next morning: Tape a piece of butcher paper to the table. Twist one strip of paper into a 3-D curley-q design (see drawing) someplace on the paper. Tape it or glue it in place. Place the other strips on the table. See what the children do. If possible do this in an area or on a table where it can be left out for a couple days to see how the children react with, use and add to the mural.

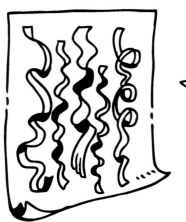

If space is a real issue, tape some paper around a cutting board or a cookie sheet. You are looking to provide a flat surface for this 3-D investigation. Be creative.

What about mounting it on the wall?

HOME MADE CLAY BEADS

Use this recipe to make clay beads for stringing and painting.

You Need: 1 cup cornstarch
2 ½ cups baking soda
1 ½ cups cold water

Hand-Eye Coordination

Small Motor Skills

Creativity

Cooking Skills

Math/Counting

Social Skills

Language Development

Following Directions

Dramatic Play

Directions:

Mix all the ingredients together in a saucepan. Cook on medium heat until thick. Keep stirring while cooking. Remove from heat, knead. Break off small chunks of the clay and roll and mold into bead shapes. Poke holes through the center of the beads with straws. Leave the straw in the bead to keep the hole open. The straws WILL NOT melt while the beads are baking. Place the beads on a cookie sheet and bake at 300° for about 45 minutes. Cool. Paint. Dry. String!

Options:

You can use tempra paint (with smaller brushes), markers or nail polish to color your dried beads!

From the Ooey Gooey® Test Kitchens:

None of the testers believed that the straws wouldn't melt. They didn't melt. They won't for you either. We promise.

FRIENDSHIP BRACELETS

You Need: Yarn or string or curly ribbon

Plastic beads (store bought at a craft store)

Directions:

Allow the children to string and exchange friendship bracelets.

Hand-Eye Coordination

Small Motor Skills

Creativity

Math/Counting

Sorting

Social Skills

Language Development

Following Directions

Dramatic Play

MASKING TAPE BRACELETS

This one is a big hit with the toddlers!

You Need: Masking Tape
Scraps of paper

Wrap a piece of masking tape
(loosely) around the child's wrist with
the sticky side facing out. Have small
scraps of paper out and available to
stick on their bracelets!

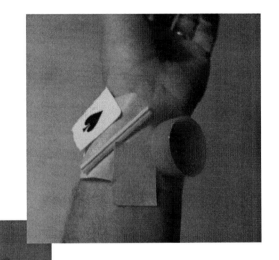

Hand-Eye Coordination

Small Motor Skills

Creativity

Math/Counting

Social Skills

Language Development

Following Directions

Dramatic Play

PAPER TOWEL TUBE BRACELETS

You Need: Paper Towel Tubes
Foil
Scissors
Small colored pastas or bits of paper and glue (optional)

Hand-Eye Coordination

Small Motor Skills

Creativity

Math/Counting

Social Skills

Language Development

Following Directions

Dramatic Play

Directions:

A former co-teacher of mine taught me this one. It's a bit more product oriented than I like, but I thought I'd include it here for you to do with it what you will.... It is definitely more of a craft. In a nutshell: you will be cutting bracelets out of the paper rolls, rounding the edges and covering the bracelets with foil. The final (and optional step) is the children to gluing some small bits of things to the bracelets.

The Specifics:

- Cut the paper towel tube into 1 ½ - 2 inch rings.
- Make 1 cut across the width of the ring, so the ring is now a strip.
- Use scissors to round the edges.
- Cover the bracelet with foil.

There you go!

MAKING PLACEMATS

You Need: Markers or Crayons
                   Paper
                   Laminating Machine

Directions:

Have the children color on a piece of paper which you will then laminate to serve as his/her individual placemat for snack and lunch time.

Creativity
Small Motor Skills
Name Recognition

WEAVING PAPER MATS

Another way of making individual placemats.

Small Motor Skills

Elements of Design

Creativity

You Need: 2 sheets of different colored construction paper
Scissors
Laminator (optional)

Directions:
Fold 1 piece of paper in half (as shown). Make vertical cuts in the paper. Open it up. Cut the second piece of paper into strips, longways. Weave the long strips through the vertical slits that you cut in the first paper. Laminate if desired.

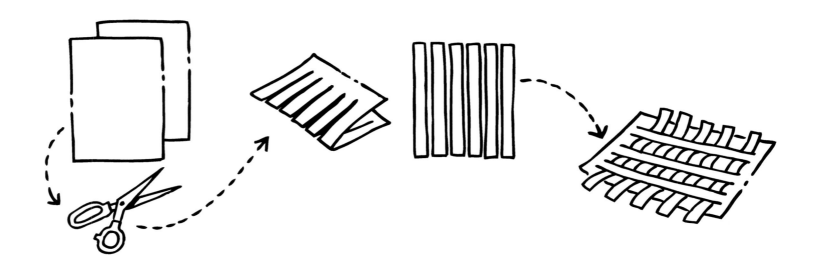

COOKED CORNSTARCH FINGER PAINT

Creativity

Self Expression

Small Motor Skills

Color Mixing

Painting

Descriptive Language

Sensory Awareness

You Need: ½ cup cornstarch
¾ cup cold water
2 cups hot water
1 TBS glycerin (makes it shiny and assists in drying)
Food coloring or liquid watercoloring

Directions:

Mix the ½ cup cornstarch and ¾ cup cold water in a saucepan. Then add the 2 cups hot water. Stir in the glycerin. Cook over medium heat, stirring frequently, for about 3-5 minutes. It will look like pudding as it starts to heat up.

Remove from the heat and carefully pour it into the containers you will be storing it in. This is when I color it with various colors of liquid water color. It is very creamy when it is hot and as it cools it continues to look like thick pudding.

It cools down in about 30 minutes. Stir it up and allow the children to fingerpaint freely with it. Allow their pictures to dry overnight. Notice that the pictures have a shiny sheen when dry. Pretty neat!

A note on paper:

If you use heavier finger-paint paper, the paper stays flat when drying. If you use regular art paper the edges curl when drying but the paint does NOT crack or come off when you smooth the paper back down.

EDIBLE FINGER PAINT

You Need: 1 big bottle of Corn Syrup
Food coloring
A few small cups or paint containers

Directions:
Divide up the corn syrup into the smaller cups. Add food coloring. Mix and paint freely with either fingers, brushes or maybe even your tongue!

Note:
Use food coloring and not liquid watercolor for this mixture because the children will tend to lick their fingers and eat some of it!

From the Ooey Gooey®
Test Kitchens:
These pictures are shiny and sticky.
They take a long time to dry.

Creativity
Self Expression
Small Motor Skills
Color Mixing
Painting
Descriptive Language
Sensory Awareness

SPARKLE PAINT

Creativity

Self Expression

Small Motor Skills

Color Mixing

Painting

Descriptive Language

Sensory Awareness

You Need: 4 cups flour (any kind)
2 cups salt
Water to desired thickness
(have 4 cups on hand but you will NOT use it all)
Liquid water color for pigment
Electric Mixer

Directions:

Mix the dry ingredients in a mixing bowl. Using an electric mixer, slowly add the water and mix it all up. Add water until you get the consistency you prefer.

This homemade paint can be used for painting with brushes, objects (like plungers or potato mashers) or even fingerpainting! It has a little sparkle when it dries. It dries very quickly and doesn't crack off the paper. It is food though, so store in an airtight container.

MARSHMALLOWS AND TOOTHPICKS

You Need: Toothpicks
Marshmallows

Directions:
Allow the children to construct 3-D designs with toothpicks and marshmallows.

Reality Check:
Some are going to build. Some are going to eat.
Some adults say, "You can eat it once you have built it."
Here's the thing – do what you need to do, and say what you need to say, just don't get so uptight about it. Really, it's OK. Besides, if you really don't want them eating the marshmallows, you shouldn't be doing this activity in the first place.

Construction

Elements of Design

Spatial Awareness

Small Motor Skills

Math/Counting

Descriptive Language (talking about their construction)

Creativity

3-D Designs

FROZEN TASTY PICTURES

Creativity

Small Motor Skills

Properties of Water

Opposites (wet/dry)

Sensory Awareness

Color Mixing

Important Note Before Starting:
You have to prepare the ice cubes the night before!

You Need: Premade ice cubes
Jello® or Kool-Aid® Powder
Paper
Popsicle Sticks

Directions:
Make ice cubes with popsicle sticks in them. Sprinkle the Jello® or Kool Aid® powder on the paper. Using the popsicle stick as a handle, move the ice cubes through the powder. This makes a yummy colorful design!

Reality Check:
Someone is going to lick the paper. Calm down. It's OK.

ICE CUBE DESIGNS

This is a variation of marble painting.

You Need: Colored ice cubes
Paper
A shallow soda box or the top of a copy paper box

Directions:
Put the paper in the box. Plop a few colored ice cubes on the paper. Shake and move the box so the ice cube rolls around on the paper.

Variation:
Freeze the colored water in egg-shaped gelatin molds. Then they will roll better because they are egg shaped!

Creativity
Color Mixing
Visual Tracking
Properties of Water
Opposites (wet/dry)
Hand-Eye Coordination
Small Motor Skills

Miscellaneous FUN

SHAPES ON SHAPES

Creativity

Self Expression

Small Motor Skills

Descriptive Language

Sensory Awareness

Shape Recognition

Math/Counting

Color/Number Recognition

Spatial Skills

Directions:

Provide big pieces of square, circle, rectangle and triangle shaped paper. Provide smaller squares, circles, rectangles and triangles. Allow the children to glue the shapes onto the shapes.

For starters I would call this "Shapes on Shapes" and would put out many choices of big shapes and many choices of smaller shapes. I would let the children put any shape onto any paper. It would be more of an assorted shape collage.

Now, IF… (and I say IF)… IF for whatever reason it's only about triangles today, then only put out triangles. Don't set out lots of shapes and then run around hollering, "NO! No! Today we are doing triangles!!" You are going to get mad, the children are going to get frustrated and what might have been an honest exploration of triangles (on the paper, in the room, in books, something brought from home, are there any outside???) is going to turn into a control battle over doing it the "right" way. Tread lightly.

Please remember too that there are shapes beyond circles, squares and triangles. There will be that one year with that one child who needs you to know the following:

Quadrilateral = 4 sides (square, rhombus, rectangle, parallelogram, trapezoid, kite)

Pentagon = 5 sides

Hexagon = 6 sides

Septagon (also called Heptagon) = 7 sides

Octagon = 8 sides

Nonagon = 9 sides

Decagon = 10 sides

Be ready!

COLORS ON COLORS

Creativity

Self Expression

Small Motor Skills

Descriptive Language

Sensory Awareness

Shape Recognition

Math/Counting

Color/Number Recognition

Spatial Skills

Directions:

Start a collection of red, orange, yellow, green, blue and purple things that can be used for color collages. I stored my collections in shoe boxes. A red box, orange box, blue box, etc.

When you have collected enough color coordinated goodies you can do **Red on Red.** Red paper with red glue and red things. Then you can do **Blue on Blue**. Blue paper with blue glue and blue things. You get the idea!

BUBBLE PAINTING AGAINST THE WALL

You Need: Individual containers of bubbles

Food coloring

Butcher Paper

Creativity

Small Motor Skills

Bubbles/Surface Tension

Air/Blowing

Math/Counting

Shapes and Colors

Descriptive Language

I find that store bought bubbles work best for this so that everyone can have their own to hold in their hand. Plus it's an easy size for the children to hold in their hands which is important for this activity. So I would suggest either buying the bubbles yourself, asking parents to each provide a bottle for their child, or maybe start saving the store bought containers and refill them with your preferred recipe of homemade bubble juice. Regardless of how you get it ready, this is what you are going to do:

Directions:

Tape a big sheet of butcher paper against the wall. Color the individual containers of bubbles with FOOD COLORING. Not liquid watercolor. For some reason the liquid water color tends to have a negative reaction with the bubble soap and sometimes de-activates the bubble solution. To be on the safe side you might want to err on the side of caution and use food coloring with this activity. Maybe do a small test run with the liquid water color (formulas tend to change!) but food coloring always works.

Then blow the bubbles on to the paper in front of you. When they pop they will leave colored bubble prints.

One of our favorites!

MARKERS ON COFFEE FILTERS

Creativity

Small Motor Skills

Descriptive Language

Chromatography

Solubility

Opposites (wet/dry)

Evaporation

Absorption

You Need: An assortment of various sizes of coffee filters

Water based markers

Water

Directions:

Color all over your coffee filter with markers.

Then put water on the coffee filter.

Watch what happens to the coffee filter.

Ways to get the water on the filters:

Squirt bottles

Plant mister

Pipettes

Turkey basters

BODY TRACING

You Need: Butcher paper
Markers
Children

Small Motor Skills

Body Awareness

Creativity

Socialization

Language Skills

Directions:

Cut sheets of butcher paper that are long enough for you to trace the children. Have the children lay down on the paper. Do they want to put their arms or legs in a funny position? One hand up? One arm down? Once they decide, trace around their body. Allow them to color their bodies.

A Creative Option:

If you have hand held or full length mirrors, move them to where the children are coloring themselves. They can look at themselves in the mirror while coloring and/or drawing.

Reality Check:

Use caution when saying things like, "Paint your shirt!" because they just might.

Variation:

Do it with chalk outside on the cement, patio, asphalt or driveway.

CARS WITH MARKERS TAPED TO THEIR BUTT

Tracking

Hand-Eye Coordination

Creativity

Small Motor Skills

You Need: Markers
Plastic cars
Masking tape
Paper

Directions:

Tape the markers to the back of the car so that when the children push the cars they will be making marks on the paper. When positioning the marker for taping, take the marker lids off to make sure it is lined up with where the paper will be. Then put the lids back on.

SHADOW TRACINGS

You Need: Chalk
Driveway or Sidewalk
A sunny day

Directions:
Have the children stand still. Funny poses optional. Trace their shadows on the ground with the chalk. Let them decorate!

For Older Children:
Stand in the same spot and in the same position every hour. Make shadow tracings each time. Observe the change in the positions of the shadows as the sun moves through the sky.

Small Motor Skills
Body Awareness
Creativity
Socialization Skills
Language Development
Math/Measurement
Shadows
Passage of Time
Movement of the Sun

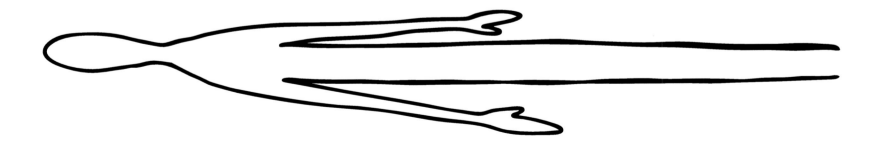

EXPLODING PICTURES

You Need: Paper towels (you will use ½ of a sheet at a time)
Sandwich sized Ziploc® baggies
Lots of baking soda (you will use 2 TBS at a time)
Gallon of vinegar (you will use 1 cup at a time)
Food coloring or liquid water coloring (to color the vinegar)
A big sheet of paper (or newspaper) to capture the explosions

Creativity

Pressure

Explosions

Carbon Dioxide

Action/Reaction

Cause/Effect

Color Mixing

Directions:
First, put a large sheet of paper on the ground. Then place the 2 TBS of baking soda in the center of the ½ square of the paper towel. Fold up the paper towel and put it in the baggie. Next, pour 1 cup of colored vinegar into the baggie and quickly close the baggie. You do not need to be in a super hurry. But you do want to do it quick! Now put the baggie down on the paper.

3-2-1 Blast Off!

What's Happening?
The pressure inside the baggie will force the bag open and the color vinegar will POP and EXPLODE out on to the paper!

For an added bonus (you will need an assistant) have a couple bags ready to go at once! Then you can watch more than one colorful explosion at the same time.

From the Ooey Gooey® Test Kitchens:
We found that the POP was more exciting than the design it made on the paper. You might find a similar reaction from the children too.

Step #1

Step #2

Step #3

SEWING PLATES

You can purchase commercially made sewing cards, but I like to make them with the children.

You Need: Hole punch

Paper plates (the thin cheap kind)

String

Masking tape

Hand-Eye Coordination
Small Motor Skills
Creativity
Use of Tools

Directions:

Fold the plate over and start punching holes in it. Cut a section of string, long enough to sew, but not so long as to frustrate and get all knotted up.

Tie one end of the string to one of the holes. Then wrap a piece of masking tape at the other end of the string for the "needle." The tape will keep the edge from fraying and will allow the children to sew through the holes you have punched.

Variation:

Punch holes in recycled holiday, greeting and birthday cards. Keep a sewing center ready if your children seem to really enjoy this activity.

True Fact:

Children can be taught to safely use a needle, thread and a square of burlap on an embroidery hoop. Do you sew?

158

SCIENCE ACTIVITIES

KNOX® GELATIN MOLDS

You Need: Knox®Gelatin
Non-stick cooking spray
Containers
Water

Creativity

Chemistry

Chemical/Physical Reactions

Cooking

Small Motor Skills

Directions:
The ratio is 3/4 cup water to 1 packet of Knox®. *Take the number of cups of water your container holds and DIVIDE by .75* This is how many packets of Knox® you need.

Before You Get Started: Spray the container(s) you are using with whatever non-stick spray you have around so it doesn't stick.

In a saucepan, heat the water over low heat, add the packets of gelatin. Stir until it dissolves. Pour the Knox® liquid into the containers and let it set overnight. Some swear by "on the counter" some prefer "put it in the fridge". The choice is yours, they will both work. They produce different textures. Play around with both until you find the one you (and the children) like best.

Once the mold is set, take it out of the container and put in your sensory tub or onto a tray. Provide pipettes and eyedroppers filled with colored water so the children can poke the colored water into the molds!

Optional Tools:
Straws
Popsicle sticks
Kitchen utensils

Variation:
See "Jelly Cake" on page 62/63

Various Suggestions of Containers:
I have used ice cube trays, bundt cake pans, angel food cake pans, various
novelty molds (I found one in the shape of a brain!), egg shaped ones, various
sizes of Tupperware®, various food storage containers. Look for square shapes,
novel shapes, tall cylindrical shapes. There is no limit to what you can use!

GRASS BALLS

You Need: An assortment of nylon stockings (knee-hi's or regular)
Potting Soil
Grass seed
A plastic or Styrofoam cup

Directions:
You will need 5 inches of nylon (measure from the toe, up). First, put about ¼ cup of grass seed in the nylon. Put about 1 ½ cups of potting soil on the top. (These amounts are estimates and do not need to be exact!) Your grass ball should be big, about 3 inches across. Tie a knot in the nylon stocking to hold the ball in place but don't cut the extra nylon "tail" off.

Now, put about 2 inches of water in your cup. Turn the grass ball so that the nylon "tail" hangs into the water. Check water levels daily and fill as needed. How long did it take before your grass-ball started growing grass-hair?

Small Motor Skills

Math/Measurement

Graphing and Charting

Opposites (wet/dry)

Evaporation

Estimating

Social Skills

Physical Changes

Dramatic Play

Language Development

Sensory Awareness

Use of Tools

IVORY® SOAP EXPLOSION

I often think this one is more for the adults than the kids!

You Need: Ivory® Soap (Lots. Trust me)
Paper Plate
Microwave

Directions:

Unwrap the paper off a bar of Ivory® Soap. Place the bar of soap in the center of the paper plate. Microwave on high for about 2 minutes.

What is happening? Ivory® Soap is filled with air. That is why it floats. When you put Ivory® Soap in the microwave the air heats up and expands. Check out that foaming reaction! Be ready to repeat. Again. And again.

Promises:

It will not ruin your microwave.

It will not make your food smell like soap for the rest of the week.

Variation:

Peeps Gone Wild!

Go through the same process using Marshmallow Peeps®.

163

ELEPHANT TOOTHPASTE

You Need: 3 or 4 empty, 20 oz. water bottles

3 or 4 bottles of hydrogen peroxide (you will use 1 ½ cups at a time)

Dish soap (any brand, but we liked how Dawn® reacted the best)

Food coloring or liquid water color (have an assortment of choices)

1 jar of yeast (you will use 2 tsp. at a time)

Warm water (you will use 3 TBS at a time)

A dish pan, water table tub or small sensory bin to contain the reaction

Chemical Reactions

Eruptions

Language Development

Small Motor Skills

Social Skills

Comparing and Contrasting

Directions:

Place the bottle in your sensory bin. Pour 1 ½ cups of hydrogen peroxide into the bottle and add a few drops of the dish soap. Add a little bit of coloring and put a funnel in the top of the bottle.

In a separate small cup dissolve the 2 tsp of yeast in 3 TBS of warm water. Pour the yeast and water mixture into the bottle, remove the funnel and check out that reaction!

Be ready to repeat this cool reaction!

MAGIC TOUCH BAGS

You Need: Ziploc® baggies
Various substances such as:

- Hair gel
- Glitter
- Shortening
- Peanut Butter
- Shaving cream
- Corn syrup
- Chocolate syrup

Small Motor Skills

Sensory Awareness

Textures

Colors

Language Develoment

Directions:

Put some corn syrup (or whatever you choose) into a baggie. Maybe add some glitter, or marbles or some food coloring or liquid water colors. Squeeze and squish. Children who do not like touching the sensory tub materials or do not like playing with shaving cream on the table will often explore it if it is contained in a "safe" container, like a Ziploc® bag.

If necessary, tape the tops of the baggies closed.

Suggestion:

Try taping a gallon sized Ziploc® with hair gel, glitter and a couple marbles inside of it, on to the table. Watch as the children strengthen those fingers when they puuuussssh those marbles through the hair gel!

CURDS AND WHEY
-OR-
MISS MUFFETT'S LUNCH

Science

Chemistry

Reactions

Language Development

Observation Skills

This recipe is often referred to as "Plastic Milk" in preschool circles. As in, *"Hey, have you ever made plastic milk?"* but the truth of the matter is that it is not plastic, it's casein. Which are curds (ie: cheese). The liquid left behind once the curds separate out is the whey.

But technicalities aside, here are the two ways of making casein that have worked best for us. Each recipe makes exactly the same amount. The difference really is microwave vs. stove top. I have included them both because I am aware of the various (yet sometimes limited) cooking options many of you have.

These two activities are more of a chemical reaction to discuss and observe, as opposed to something you would make and "play with." They are both definitely a science based activity example of "process vs. product."

Curds and Whey (Stovetop)

You Need: 1 cup milk
2 tsp. vinegar

Directions:
Put the milk and vinegar in a saucepan. Cook and stir over medium heat until it slowly starts to boil. The lumps (curds) will start to separate out from the liquid

(whey). Strain the whey into a small cup or bowl and scoop the curds on to a plate or into a bowl as well. There you have it. Curds and whey. Looks a little like cottage cheese doesn't it?

Curds and Whey (Microwave)

You Need: 1 ½ cups milk
4 tsp vinegar

Directions:
Put the milk and vinegar in a microwave safe container. I like a large, microwave safe measuring cup so the children can see the reaction as it occurs. Cook on high heat for about 1 minute. Depending on the heat levels of your microwave, you will either have the curds and whey after a minute of cooking, or you will need to do it again. The separation of liquid and solid is pretty obvious, so you will be able to tell if it needs another minute or not.

Once the liquid and solid are obviously separated, strain the whey into a small cup or bowl and scoop the curds on to a plate or into a bowl as well. There you have it. Curds and whey.

Note:
Both the curds and whey are safe to "taste" if someone wants to try them, unless of course they have a dairy allergy.

LIQUID LAYERS II: THE SEQUEL

This appeared in *The Ooey Gooey® Handbook* but we have since had other great ideas of liquids suggested, so we'll call this one Liquid Layers II: The Sequel.

Science

Density

Color Recognition

Observation Skills

Small Motor Skills

Language Development

You Need: Clear plastic party cups

Various liquids from the suggestions listed below

The original suggested liquids:

Pink shampoo

Blue dish soap

Colored water (we used green)

Cooking oil (yellow)

New to the suggested line up:

Olive Oil (yellow)

Baby Oil (Clear)

Mineral Oil (clear)

Hot Pepper Oil (Orange)

Corn Syrup (clear-ish)

Glycerine (clear)

Balsamic Vinegar (black)

Rubbing Alcohol (clear)

Directions:

Choose three or four of the liquids suggested here and pour them into your cup. Now pour the same liquids into a second cup, but pour them in a different order. Notice that regardless of the order you pour them in, they will separate out the same way and in the same order because of their various (yet consistent) densities.

EDIBLE FAKE BARF

You Need: Applesauce (Get a big jar, you will use ½ cup at a time)
Raisin Bran Cereal
Oatmeal
Cocoa Power (optional)
Unflavored Gelatin (you will use 2 packets for each batch of barf)

Directions:

In a frying pan heat ½ cup of applesauce. Add two packets of gelatin. Mix until the gelatin is dissolved in the applesauce. If you are using the optional cocoa powder you would add it at this point. Then add some oatmeal and some raisin bran to make it look like chunky barf. Stir. Remove from heat. Spread the barf out on plate until it has the look you desire. Allow it cool completely then remove it from the plate with a spatula.

You can eat it. Gross.

I know that everything is a learning experience, but there has to be one thing we include for the pure pleasure and intrigue of it…. This one is it. Sorry WOLVES, this one is just for the sheer joy of it!

From the Ooey Gooey® Test Kitchen:

We made one batch with the cocoa powder and one without. The one without cocoa powder looked more like vomit. The chocolate one, well, it kind of looked like something else. I am sure a room full of three-year olds will be more than happy to tell you what they think it looks like.

We tasted them both. They were not great. I enjoyed making it, but don't necessarily plan on eating it again.

We left them on the counter overnight and they both were fine to use the next day as well. This one will definitely be a hit in your room and at your next birthday party!

MASKING TAPE ROAD

You Need: Masking Tape
Toy Cars
A Wall (or floor or a long piece of paper)

Directions:
I peeked in the window of the toddler room one afternoon and noticed that they had made a masking tape road on the wall. The children (who had previously been zooming cars all over the walls anyway) now had a route to follow.

Note:
If you use "blue tape" (painter's tape) it won't peel the paint off your walls.

Variation:
Draw a road with markers on a big long sheet of butcher paper and tape that to the wall. Be sure to tape it up on the wall at their height, not yours.

Make a road (out of paper or tape) on the floor.

Small Motor Skills

Social Skills

Visual Tracking

Descriptive Language

Opposites (fast/slow)

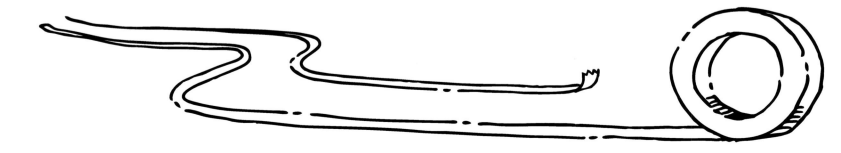

WALL BRAIDING

You Need: Towel rings
Yarn
Ability to braid

Creativity
Small Motor Skills
Language Development
Hand-Eye Coordination

Directions:
Mount the towel rings at the child's height. Loop the yarn over the ring and tie it at the top so it doesn't come off the ring. Braid with the yarn that is hanging off the ring.

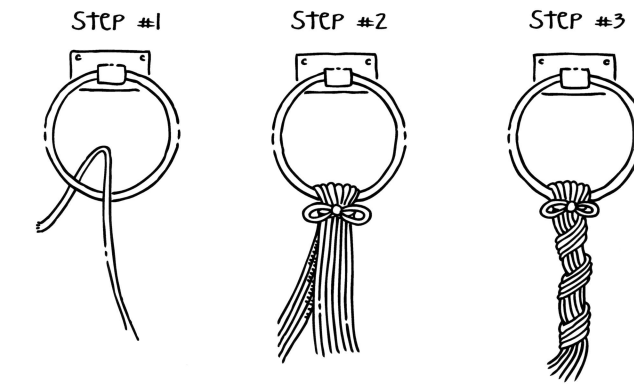

Step #1   Step #2   Step #3

PAPER PLAY MONEY

You Need: Scissors
Green construction paper

Directions:
Cut out green construction paper in the shape of rectangles. Call it "money." It is fascinating to see what the children do with it and how they use it.

Number Recognition

Math/Counting

"More Than"

"Less Than"

Economics

Dramatic Play

FLOWER ARRANGING

You Need: Floral Foam (about $1.50 a chunk at craft stores)
Silk or plastic flowers

Directions:
The children can arrange the flowers in the floral foam.

Creativity

Spatial Skills

Small Motor Skills

Language Development

Math/Counting

MAKE A ZINGER

You Need: String

Foil

Cotton

Creativity

Spatial Skills

Small Motor Skills

Language Development

Problem Solving

Directions:

When compiling this book for you I plowed through my old lesson planning books. From way back in 1993 I found this: Give each child a 10" piece of string, 2 squares of foil and a cotton ball and this simple instruction: "Make a Zinger!"

Now it's your turn. Go make a Zinger!

From the Ooey Gooey® Test Kitchen:

A couple testers wanted to know how big of a piece of foil. I told them to make it as big as they thought they needed it to be in order to make a Zinger....

CEREAL STACKING

This has always been one of our favorites.

You Need: Froot Loops® or Cheerios® cereal
(or any kind of ring-shaped cereal)
Playdough
Raw spaghetti

Directions:

Roll up a small (but not tiny) ball of playdough.

Stick it on a tray or right on the table.

Put a piece of raw spaghetti in it so the spaghetti is sticking straight up.

Stack the cereal onto the spaghetti sticks.

Creativity
Spatial Skills
Small Motor Skills
Language Development
Math/Counting

179

SHAVING CREAM SHAVINGS

You Need: Shaving Cream
Mirrors
Popsicle Sticks

Creativity

Small Motor Skills

Language Development

Dramatic Play

Directions:

The children can put shaving cream on their face and "shave" with popsicle sticks while looking at themselves in the mirror.

SHAVING CREAM AND BLOCKS

You Need: Smaller size table-top blocks
Shaving cream
Popsicle sticks

Directions:

The children can stack big block towers on top of the table while using shaving cream as "cement".

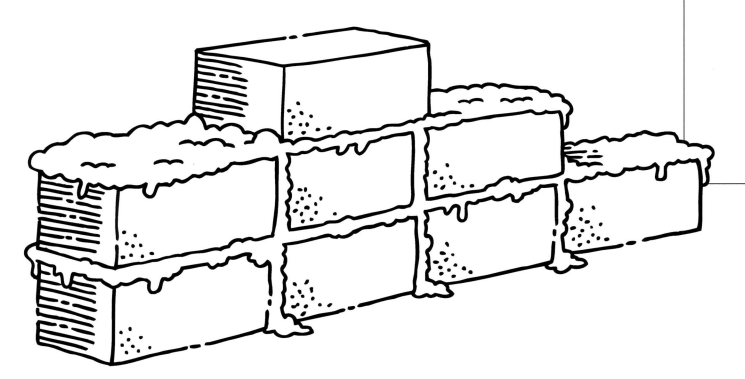

Small Motor Skills
Spatial Skills
Construction
Elements of Design
Gravity
Math/Counting
Balance
Estimating
Sensory Awareness

CON-TACT® PAPER, BEANS AND RICE

Creativity

Small Motor Skills

Language Development

Math/Counting

You Need: Con-Tact® Paper

Dried pinto beans

Small squares of colored paper

Rice (colored or not)

Directions:

Cut out rectangle shapes of Con-Tact® Paper. Peel the paper backing off to expose the sticky side. Tape the Con-Tact® Paper *sticky side up* on top of the table. Have small containers of beans, rice and bits of paper. The children ca stick the beans, rice and paper pieces onto the Con-Tact® Paper.

STYROFOAM CHUNKS AND GOLF TEES

You Need: A chunk of Styrofoam™ (or Floral Foam)
Golf Tees

Directions:

Allow the children to push golf tees into big chunks of Styrofoam™ or Floral Foam.

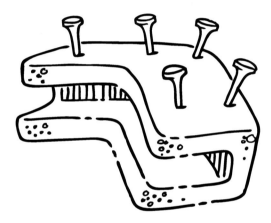

Creativity

Spatial Skills

Small Motor Skills

Language Development

Math/Counting

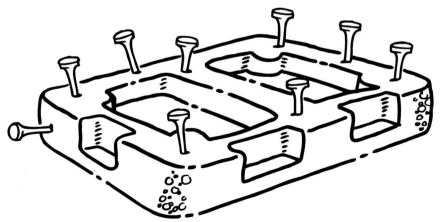

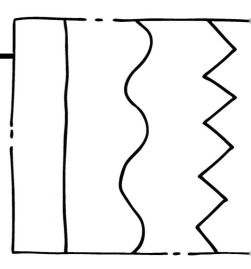

CUTTING STRIPS

You Need: Paper
Markers
Scissors

STEP #1

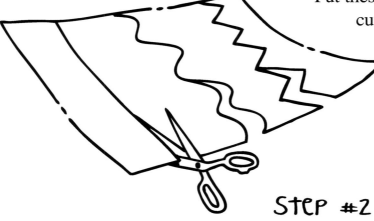

Directions:

2 ways to make these: 1) draw the lines on the back of scratch paper 2) draw the lines on one sheet of paper and make copies. Your choice.

On a piece of paper draw three lines:
One straight line
One curvy line
One zig-zag line

Put these papers out on the table with some scissors. The children can cut on the lines.

Reality Check:

Some children will cut on the pre-drawn lines. Some will not. It's OK.

STEP #2

Creativity
Small Motor Skills
Math/Counting
Following Directions
Hand-Eye Coordination

MAGNET BOARD

You Need: Oil Drip Pan
Magnets

Creativity
Small Motor Skills
Language Development
Math/Counting
Science/Magnetics
Comparing and Contrasting

Directions:
Get an oil drip pan from the automotive section of your favorite store. They are big. They typically go under the car in the garage. You are going to use it to make a big magnet board in your classroom. You don't have to do anything to it. Just prop it up against the wall and place a box, bin or tray of magnets in front of it. A magnet board!

Option:
You can mount it to the wall if you want.

Suggestion:
When you go shopping for your oil drip pan, be sure to bring a magnet with you so you can MAKE SURE it really is magnetic!

A T-SHIRT CAPE

You Need: T-shirt
Scissors

Directions:
You are going to make three cuts in your shirt:

1) Cut off the *sleeves* of the T-shirt (save the sleeves to make bean bags see next page).

2) Cut up the *sides* of the T-shirt.

3) Cut off the *front* of the T-shirt but leave the neckband intact.

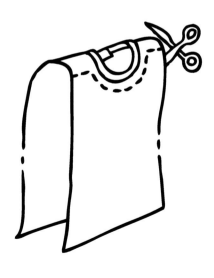

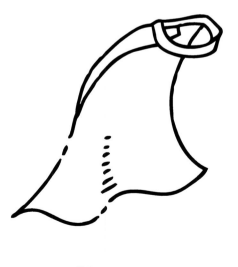

STEP #1 & 2

STEP #3

STEP #4

A BEAN BAG FROM THE SLEEVES

You Need: Filler for the bean bag
Needle and thread
The cut off sleeves of your T-Shirt cape(s)
Scissors

Directions:
Your cut off T-shirt sleeve has two closed sides and two open sides. Turn the sleeve inside-out and stitch one of the open sides closed. Now stitch *half* of the other open side closed. Turn the stitched sleeve right-side-out again and fill it with styrofoam bead filler, beans, rice or flax seed. Stitch or sew the small opening closed and there you go! You made a bean bag.

A TANGLE FREE YARN STORAGE SYSTEM

You Need: Empty, clean, dry 2-litre soda bottle
Scissors
Duct tape
Skein of yarn

Directions:
Cut the bottle in half and put the skein of yarn inside. Pull one end of the yarn through the top of the bottle. Tape the bottle back together. Now you can pull the yarn through the top of the bottle and have knot-free yarn available at all times!

SPONGE BALLS

To Make 1 You Need:

    2 rectangle shaped sponges

    Dental Floss

    Scissors

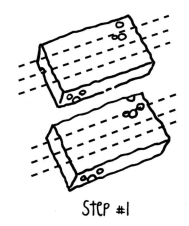

Step #1

Cheat Sheet:

To make 10 you will need 20 sponges.

To make 20 you will need 40 sponges.

Directions:

Cut each sponge into four long pieces. Stack the strips on top of each other so that you have two layers of four sponge strips. Tie a piece of dental floss around the sponges, pull tightly and knot it. There you have a sponge ball. Use it for painting, in the water table or as water balloon substitutes!

Step #2

Getting Fancy:

Get colored sponges and alternate the colored strips when you stack them up.

Step #3

DOUBLE BRUSHES

You Need: 2 Paintbrushes
Duct tape
Metal coat hanger (get them donated from the dry cleaners)
Masking tape

Directions:

Cut off a corner of the hanger so you have a big V shape. Attach one brush to each end of the V using masking tape to hold it in place. Now use the duct tape to tape the whole thing together, covering the V and the top part of the brush handle. You now have a huge V shaped double brush!

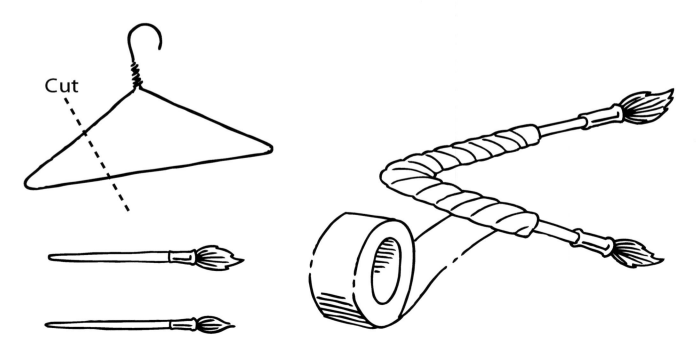

NEWSPAPER BRUSHES

To Make 1 Brush You Need:

2 full sheets of newspaper
Scissors
Masking Tape

Directions:

Open the newspaper all the way. Put the two pieces of paper on top of each other. Fold the bottom edge of the paper up to the top edge. It should look like a l-o-n-g rectangle. Now fold one side over to the other side. You should have a smaller rectangle. With your scissors make vertical cuts along the top ⅓ of the paper. Starting at one edge of the rectangle, tightly roll up your paper. Hold it closed with a couple pieces of masking tape. Gently fluff the cut edges.

Now go paint!

Step #1   Step #2   Step #3

Suggestion:
One is not enough! Once you get the hang of making them, make a bunch so you can always have a handful available.

Reality Check:
Some children will use the newspaper brushes for something else. Over the years I have seen cheerleader pom-poms, feather dusters and even tails!

Step #4   Step #5   Step #6

SHOE TYING CENTER

You Need: Shoes with laces
A piece of plywood
Hammer
Nails

Direction:

Nail the shoe to the board.   Use the mounted shoe to practice tying and lacing.

FANCY FRAMES

An idea for decorating picture frames or the magnetic frames you can put on the front of the refrigerator.

You Need: Photo Frames
Glue
Buttons
Puzzle Pieces

Directions:
Glue buttons all around the edge of the photo frame. Add the caption, "Cute as a button!"

Glue small puzzle pieces around the edge of the frame. Add the caption, "I love you to pieces!"

HOW DO I LOVE THEE? LET ME COUNT THE WAYS: EIGHT WAYS OF BUBBLE WRAP!

Or, as they called it in Amsterdam, bubelplasstic.

1. Wrap yourself in bubble wrap, let the children paint on it. Carefully get down on a big sheet of paper and roll around.

2. Put a long strip of bubble wrap on the wall for popping with your hands. Or elbows. Or thumbs.

3. Put a long strip of bubble wrap down low along the wall for popping. The children will have to lay down on their backs and pop it with their feet.

4. Put a long strip of bubble wrap down on the floor for jumping up and down on and popping with their feet.

5. You can paint and make prints with the bubble wrap regardless of where you place it!

6. Put a long strip of bubble wrap on the table for popping.

7. Tape it up to the underside of the table for popping.

8. Put a long strip of bubble wrap outside on the bike path for riding bikes over.

196

HANDPRINTS POEM #1

Sometimes you get discouraged
because I am so small
and always leave my fingerprints
on furniture and walls.

But every day I'm growing!
I'll be grown up someday
and all those tiny handprints
will surely fade away.

So here's one final handprint
just so you can recall
exactly how my fingers looked
when I was very small.

HANDPRINTS POEM #2

When I'm big you won't remember the mud I tracked on stairs.

Instead I hope that you will hear my laugh that eased your cares.

The smudges that I leave on walls will someday fade away.

But the memories of my first steps will be cherished every day.

As for these two handprints, someday you will be glad

we took some time to make a mess that didn't make you mad.

198

HANDPRINTS POEM #3

Tiny handprints grow so fast
Their awkward groping soon will clasp
A ball, a book, a sweetheart's hand
A diploma, briefcase, wedding band.

Tiny handprints grow so strong
It doesn't take them very long
To snap a shirt, to paint, to draw,
To labor hard, to drive a car.

Tiny handprints grow to be
A person that is quite unique
A wonderful mix of so many things
With his (her) own feelings, thoughts and dreams.

Tiny handprints grow to rely
On his (her) parents to bring him up just right
His (Her) parents pray that when (s)he's grown
(S)He'll say their job has been well done.

Tiny handprints are ours to love
The sweetest gift from God above
A miracle that never is surpassed
How sad they grow up way too fast.

INDEX OF ACTIVITY IDEAS